Saint-Malo

Bartizan, Cavalier Bastion. In the distance, the National Fort.

Daniel Gélin

Jean Mounier / André Lespagnol

Saint-Malo

Translated by Angela Moyon
Photographs by Hervé Boulé

ÉDITIONS OUEST-FRANCE
13 rue du Breil, Rennes

S******* aint-Malo, an obligatory port of call on any voyage to far-distant shores and part of any dream of adventure, does not reveal its ******* delights and character to all and sundry.

To get to know it well takes daring and modesty, patience and curiosity. There are those who have tried, and have claimed to have penetrated the very soul of the town in just a few days; they, like Stendhal, have carried away nothing but two or three clumsy cliches.

The town only gives as much as it receives, and the people themselves jealously guard their own love story with it, endlessly finding something new as their emotions and passions change.

Daniel Gélin, an "F.P." of the high school in Saint-Malo, who was already embodying our new sense of romanticism on the silver screen when we were but callow youths, gives us the key to "his" Saint-Malo.

His will join the others on our keyring. All of them open the secretive, walled town to those who do not yet know it well. For those who are old friends, they offer a new way of seeing it.

Jean Mounier and André Lespagnol also offer us their pointers to the community. They may be more academic but they bear the hallmarks of a long, and very close, relationship with our town.

To all three of them, Saint-Malo would like to express its gratitude for their recognition.

René Couanau
M.P. Mayor of Saint-Malo

Daniel Gélin

The Môle des Noires breakwater with the Grand-Bé and
Petit-Bé islands in the background.

The Saint-Malo of my younger years

****
I
****
    t is possible that, for some readers, this homage to Saint-Malo may occasionally seem to take on the appearance of fragmentary personal memoirs.

    I have always felt the need, from a very early age but with increasing intensity as time passed, to become at one with space and I wished to recount this most unique of places with lucidity and frankness. Because of this, I have tended to tell my own story. It could hardly be otherwise. So evident and deep was the osmosis that developed between the character of the town and history on the one hand and my adolescence on the other, that period of alchemy when one's character is finally formed, when destinies are prepared and one's personal future fashioned, that it would have been an act of treachery and total ingratitude to deny it.

The "local lad" is not necessarily lucky; sometimes it is not until much later in life, by a process of comparison, that he will realise the wonder and splendour of his past. A person born in 1921 like me, but in Saint-Malo, who took his first few faltering steps within the safety of the hard, damp sand on its beach, or in the shelter of the garden not far from the ever-present, familiar sea, who spent his childhood against the apparently banal background of the shores of the great ocean that almost entirely encircles the walled town, threateningly approaching its shores and scrutinizing the tides, then who ran or strolled along the quaysides where the usual masts swung like a pendulum and the cargo ships and trawlers lay dozing, or through the alleyways and along the esplanades of the walled town, along the ramparts that reassuringly dominate the estuary and the sea, cannot, as I have, experience the enchantment and sense of wonder that invites such homage. Let me

The Privateers' Town seen from outside the harbour.

not be categorical, however. I have no doubt that tides ebb and flow in the mysterious depths of certain souls when they first blossom forth.

It was at the age of ten, in September 1931, that I arrived in Saint-Malo with my family - my father, my mother and my sister, Monique (two years younger than me) in a Renault Monoquatre.

I was born in Angers in the working class district around the Bessonneau factory, a large plant that has since disappeared, but which used to specialise in the manufacture of anything related at that time to cables, canvas, and nets. In addition to supplying other businesses that made use of these goods, one of the most important sectors was maritime trade and, more especially, the fishing fleets that sailed to the Grand Banks off Newfoundland and near Greenland. The company provided the canvas for the sails of the last three-masters and the nets for the first trawlers.

My father, who came from a large family of very modest means in a hamlet in the Département of Deux-Sèvres, had obtained an important job in this factory. Despite his poor upbringing, a weighty course of study aimed at taking him into an ecclesiatical career had enabled him to acquire not only his humanism and taste for initiative but also wide-ranging general knowledge, which made him eminently suitable for retraining in a responsible post in management or trade.

He met my mother, a seasonal worker in this same factory. She was born in Rostrenen, a large village in the heart of Brittany, but had fled home to escape from the austere upbringing imposed by her father, François Le Mener, the local Mayor and a baker by trade, a widower with six daughters and the soul of a bard.

My life in Angers was as uneventful and peaceful as the countryside itself. I followed a banal course of study in the Lycée David d'Angers, of which I have only the vaguest memories. Apart, that is, from a genuine liking for my teachers, and boundless admiration for Jean Commère, a pupil of my own age who could already draw like an adult and who was to become one of the greatest figurative artists of our time.

Sometimes, in the empty streets around the factory, linen or cotton would flutter gently through the air like snowflakes, giving the street an dreamlike atmosphere. And I can still hear the brief calls of the pedlars.

Winter Sundays were like winter Sundays anywhere in the provinces. They were peaceful, consisting mainly of modest fare and contemplative strolls, like the one which provided me with the background for my dreams, around the Plantagenets' castle that was very rightly nicknamed "World's End". My mother, a genius in the kitchen and a lover of tales of mystery, would tell us the legends of her native

With my sister, Monique.

Brittany, filled with familiar ghosts and saintly miracle-workers who were already fashioning my taste for the extraordinary.

For the summer holidays, my parents used to rent a modest house not far from Angers. After crossing the Pont Domnacus that spanned the R. Loire, we would head for Erigné, then for Le Pont de Cé.

The house, standing in its own garden, was separated from the river by a narrow road and a few fields. In the summer months, the Loire ebbs at will. In some places, its level falls so low that fine sandbanks appear, an ideal place for children to enjoy themselves. These sandspits were surrounded by water, some of it still deep in places yet, foolishly, we used to swim in its clear fresh lazily-running flow.

The holidays were lively but uneventful. Dinners beneath the acacia bower blended the aromas of the meal with the sweet garden scents that grew more pronounced as evening progressed.

Nearby, I could sense the presence of the indomitable yet languid R. Loire. These early childhood years were filled with great tenderness. I grew up, unhurried and patient, amidst the legendary delicacy of Anjou.

Then everything changed. My father was appointed to Saint-Malo as his factory's representative. This was a huge step up the ladder for him, a source of minor anxiety for my mother, and a reason for immense joy on the part of my sister and myself, for we felt instinctively that, at last, something was going to happen in our lives.

Saint-Malo ! Saint-Malo, a name that conjured up so many legends and adventures in our young minds. We arrived directly on the Place de la Fontaine, opening onto the Sillon and running along the length of the endless beach from which the (to us) unknown smell of the ozone and seaweed assailed our nostrils to the Duguay-Trouin Basin on whose jetties stood my father's "dock-warehouses", the scene of intense activity at this time of the year. We could see the unique combination of vegetable farmers' transport, carts drawn by mighty Percheron horses, filled to overflowing with cauliflowers, potatoes and artichokes, and lorries or handcarts full of coils of rope, canvas and nets. There were sailors, often none too steady on their feet, and thirsty dockers who went from wharfside buildings to smoke-ridden bars. The superb three-masters, with their sails furled, lay side by side with the tall trawlers, still bearing the scars of storms, emptying their bellies of cargoes of flat, dried salt cod that was set out on great trays swung through the air by the skilful, methodical, metal cranes.

The atmosphere was noisy; it had all the feverish activity of returns from the sea and landings, with luxurious or rough cargoes that were the reward for so much effort, brought home after so many dangers and battles fought in the midst of implacable storms, banks of ice, and indecisive mists that carried with them the"ankou" ("Death" in Breton).

I was to return to the quaysides time and again to watch what was going on.

I was ten years old. Exhausted ships and mariners conjured up pictures for me of Newfoundland, and scenes from the northernmost climes.

My feet waded through the doubtful whiteness of salt crystals.

Across the square, the sea that had given rise to all this activity seemed, on that first day at least, to be relaxing; it had drawn far out from the shore, leaving its beach uncovered, and deserted on this autumn day. We lived on the second floor of a house at the corner of the Place de la Fontaine and the Sillon. From the top of the double-glazed windows, I had an even better view of this immense expanse of water stretching from Paramé to the right, in the nor'west, to the extreme left, to the south-west where, massive within its ring of granite, its belltower jutting up like a mast among the tall privateers' houses, like a challenge or a proud, sacred salute to sky and sea, the fabulous walled town, the "Cité", seemed to be waiting for me.

June 1933.

17

The groynes along the main beach.

I was enrolled in the secondary school immediately, a school that was famous for the quality of its teaching. Many of the pupils came from all over Western France; they were the sons of tradesmen or farmers. They, of course, were boarders. The others lived within the walled town or outside it and were, therefore, day pupils, like me. The school had many vocations but, in those days, it had two particular aims viz. to prepare pupils for careers in the Navy and the Church, in particular among the missionary orders.

Without too much ostentation, we were being prepared to take to the sea and convert the infidel. The school buildings were inside the walled town, on higher ground to the north-west, near St. Vincent's Cathedral.

I used to walk to school along the Sillon, the promenade. Sometimes, I walked along the beach, strolling past the groynes. I then reached a sort of slash in the granite wall, just before the headland on which the castle stood. But I avoided this sloping breach, into which the sea rolled, at low tide when seaweed-gatherers used it as an access to and from the beach.

I still have a very vivid memory of the carts loaded with streaming brown algae drawn by several percheron horses, slithering and tripping over the slabs beneath the whips of the wildly-shouting farmers.

I then entered the town by St. Vincent's Gate. It was by this famous gateway that I first discovered Saint-Malo.

I was immediately struck by an indefinable impression which has never faltered as time passes, the feeling of entering a closed, yet inhabited, almost haunted universe. A feeling that is both pagan and sacred but in which I sensed, once I had left the Place Châteaubriand on my right and reached the streets that resemble alleyways because of the height of the houses, the rare combination of wordless poetry, written by legend, history and bustling or contemplative everyday life in which I was henceforth privileged to participate. In the streets was the same activity; it was, perhaps, slightly less dense in the neighbouring alleys. There were seafarers from every corner of the world whose ship was tied up in the harbour, fair-haired men from Nordic climes, weatherbeaten dark-haired men, strong cargo hold labourers, fishermen dressed in yellow oilskins, elegantly-dressed officers, long-haul captains dressed in navy blue, Englishmen wearing tweeds or trench coats, and laughing Africans who were delighted to have some time ashore. My head spun, I was fascinated by this mixture of languages from every country, and the mixture of social classes and races that can be seen in any port was more noticeable here because of

The Sillon promenade and the tramway stop.

the narrowness of the street that climbed to the right, to the square in front of the cathedral, or branched off to the left, to the Dinan Gate. I may have been very young but I was already aware of the extent to which the women, though few in number, were beautiful and different, the subject of mute homage in the eyes of passers-by, almost all of them men of the sea. Adventurers. The women still had the golden tan left behind by the summer months. There were blonds with pale eyes, or brunettes with a bright blue gaze, the delightful descendents of Nordic or Spanish ancestors, some of whom travelled here from very far afield.

After my period of wandering, rubbing shoulders with the crowd, with the mystery of the adjacent streets, esplanades, hidden recesses, and slopes, after a vague feeling of discomfort as I passed the brothels steeped in sinfulness, after the sense of imprisonment described by Stendhal, an open-air imprisonment lightened by the cries of the seagulls indicating the nearness of the sea, I felt the pull, almost a tangible need, to undertake a "tour of the walls".

On most occasions, I started my almost ritual stroll at the St. Vincent Gate and set off southwards. There are those who declare that it is easy to see the various ages in the building of these ramparts. At that age I knew nothing of the tumult of History and the unique, cyclomythical destiny of the walled town; I felt, on the contrary, a uniformity and harmony that was little short of miraculous.

Place Chateaubriand.

The St. Vincent Gate.

The town walls stretch from the St. Vincent Gate to the St. Philip Bastion, passing the Main Gate flanked by two towers containing the statue of the Virgin Mary that protects the town, and on to the Saint-Louis Bastion and Dinan Gate. They were designed by Vauban, and built under the supervision of an architect named Garangeau when Louis XIV decided to expand the Compagnie des Indes.

This section, the so-called "noble" part of the walls, is exceptionally wide. From there, looking outwards, I could see the castle jutting out into the Sillon, the Duguay-Trouin Basin, the great avenue leading to the railway station, then the Vauban Basin where a few yachts were moored. Beyond them was the wharf used for large cargo ships; there were even a few three-masters bobbing at rest.

The ramparts and the Bidouane Tower.

Inside the town walls.

The Cavalier Bastion seen from the walls.

Looking inwards, I was impressed by the tall houses with their immense roofs, the mansions of the influential old shipowning families who, from their homes, could contemplate the comings-and-goings on the jetty, and oversee the loading and preparation of their mighty trading vessels or privateering ships. Between these grandiose mansions, I caught sight of the street running from the gates to the heart of the town, the cathedral. It is at this point on the town walls that the might of the local people can be appreciated to the full, along with the genius of the architects who designed this combination of massive walls and tall houses facing south, i.e. sheltered from strong winds and from the enemies who arrived from west and north.

Once I reached the breakwater stretching out beyond the Saint-Philip Bastion, I could see Saint-Servan in the distance, and the immense rock of Alet, a natural fortress that seems to indicate the gash carved out by the Rance Estuary.

I cannot say whether, in those days, I was really aware of the history of this place but I knew that it was steeped in legend, and I thought it marvellously beautiful.

A mysterious monk named Aaron from Scotland or Ireland is said to have settled in Alet during the first century of the Christian era; opposite, stood a rocky islet that was to attract his follower, St. Maclou. This Maclou, or Malo, is the real founder of the town. He came from Lancarvan in Wales and was the godson and follower of the Irish saint, Brandan, also known as "Brandan the Navigator" who, I like to think, discovered America some ten centuries before Christopher Columbus.

Malo, like his master, had opened his heart to God and his spirit to the sea. So this spot did indeed have a sacred origin and whatever is built, destroyed and changed here, it remains an island - and an island that is so miraculously situated that the telluric and maritime power of its origins can still be felt today.

In fact for me, at this point along the town walls and, indeed, from the point of departure, the visit that I was to undertake so often in later years and that I shall continue to undertake to my dying day cannot be described by the debonair term "stroll", for it has a ritualistic character. Whatever the time of day, and whether the tide is on the ebb or the flow, I can feel the energy produced in this estuary by the great coming and going of the ocean as it enters the wide open continent, at the spot where the Rance, with an enormous thrust forward, gives itself up to the open sea. Increasingly, in plighting my troth with the cosmos, I have the impression that certain privileged places in the universe contain eternal movements that obey the great clock among the stars, places where certain souls experience a sense of perfect harmony amidst apparent antagonism which is, on the contrary, a divine and sensual form of complicity.

Monique and me.

26

Thereafter comes the more profane contemplation of the opposite shoreline - Dinard, a resort whose elegance and naturally aristocratic geographical layout can be seen even from a distance, whether it is shrouded in sunlight or fog. Beyond it come the neighbouring villages and landscapes, fading into the horizon over the crest of the ultimate headland, the impressive bold Cap Fréhel, outlined in a purple-tinged light.

The Solidor Tower.

As my thoughts and steps wandered, I did not realise that I had reached what the locals call "Holland", a sort of garden-esplanade a few steps up above the town walls that narrow considerably at this point.

At the foot of the ramparts, which are particularly high here and where (as I noticed in later years) the cracks in the vulnerable walls are filled with shivering, silvery tufts of maritime cineraria, lies Bon-Secours Beach. At low tide, you can walk out to the Grand-Bé, an enormous mass of rock that is famous as the site of Chateaubriand's tomb. Further out to sea are the Petit-Bé, a more modest rock to the right, then the Ile Harbour and, on the horizon, the island of Cézembre. I spent hours on the promontory formed by the Holland Bastion and all that I learnt from the open sea, like a call from On High, I learnt here. I watched the ships sailing out to sea; the finest of them all were, of course, the three-masters with all sails unfurled, but there were also trawlers and cargo boats of all sizes heading for the harbour or foreign lands. All took care to avoid the numerous reefs, many of them beneath the waves, others cutting through the surface, most of them causing currents depending on the tides.

I came here often, to widen my visual horizons and the scope of my inner soul, to clear away doubts and settle difficult questions, overcome feelings of sluggishness, sorrow, fears. In fact, I came here as others go to pray in the dim light of a church. I was not only strengthened, heartened, and purified here; I was also filled with a great love of every being in the universe, all the peoples of the world, every race, with their cities, estuaries, values and collective souls.

This, of course, is where I acquired my love of travelling. It was always during the highest tides or on the stormiest of windy days that I felt the almost physical presence of God, but in fact I dreamt constantly of ports of call, harbours filled with milling crowds of people like myself, wandering aimlessly, suffering, all of them different, all of them with different religious backgrounds.

With friends.

I received a call to travel to horizons far afield, to places where I could meet such people, appreciate them, and perhaps already subconsciously learn to understand them better, resemble them, even be their re-embodiment.

I have visited nearly every port of call of which I used to dream as I sat at the top of the Holland Bastion. I have derived the very essence of men and women there. How right I was to feel instinctively that other children like me, elsewhere in the world, were perhaps also dreaming of departure, communion with others, and that invigorating virtue, the greater Fraternity which survives and improves after every storm thrown at us by the heavens, the sea and humanity itself!

The Holland Bastion and the roadstead.

I did not forget the Grand-Bé and the tomb (later deemed ostentatious but, I have to admit, excellent as a tourist attraction) of the great Chateaubriand whose glory is scarcely dimmed by such obvious opportunism, whose honour is reflected in every inhabitant of Saint-Malo and every great French writer.

Then I reached the Bidouane Tower which was, so they say, very useful during the wars with England and Holland. War has never fascinated me, quite the reverse, but I have to say that, in certain places, what man has built and designed with such great genius in order to protect cities and nations has been turned into places of observation which, for me with my love of open spaces and distant horizons, have become sanctuaries that are particularly suitable for contemplation and meditation.

Before ending my stroll, I would look further to the right, to the National Fort which is only easily accessible at low tide. Then my gaze would look to a great image of peace at very low tide - the seemingly endless beach that stretches to Rothéneuf, the scene of so much fun and so many invigorating games.

Chateaubriand's tomb on Grand-Bé.

The "Tour of the Town Walls" was finished but, instead of going through St. Thomas' Gate, I would set off to the left, towards the Place Chateaubriand where, opposite the two large, famous hotels, stands the 15th-century castle built for the Dukes of Brittany. It has occupied a prominent place in the town's history. It is not so much an inhabitable castle as a fortress built to maintain law and order in a tiny island that was, even in those days, already the home of men with strong characters. It consists of four towers connected by curtain walls.

When I was a child, I thought that, seen from outside St. Vincent's Gate, it was a wonderful sight. I learnt that, for many centuries, it was surrounded by a moat filled by the sea.

At school, life passed fairly pleasantly. Much attention was paid to teaching me my catechism and the story of Christ, and the example He set us strengthened me in a faith that was already well-anchored.

My father wanted me to become a better Christian before my first communion, which I prepared with passionate interest. For a whole year, I lived in a state of continual fervour. At one time, I even considered the idea of becoming a priest, on condition that I could take charge, not of a parish in which everything was a question of mere ritual and habit, but in a far-off land full of foreign colour. One week before the communion, the new communicants were handed over to a priest who was not on the staff of the school for a veritable retreat. The priest set us a peerless example. I nourished my soul with readings from the catechism. Between classes and frequent prayers, we were allowed to go for walks, often along the town walls.

Somersaults on the beach.

The National Fort.

The Small Keep.

The castle entrance and keep.

I felt quite different to my classmates who seemed to me to lack fire and fervour. This retreat, which I have never regretted, was one of my first experiences of "conditioning" and by the end of it, I was in such a state of mysticism that, on the eve of my first communion, I requested permission to sleep in my mother's bed because I was afraid that Christ was going to appear before me!

Apart from this crisis, I led a placid life. I had friends. Here, as anywhere else, there were gangs which I refused to join. At that time, my closest friends were the local children. I enjoyed playing football, and at school, this was obligatory. We usually played on the Eventail Beach, where Chateaubriand had walked. Some of our teachers used to let off steam with us. They had no hesitation in tucking up their cassocks so that they could dribble the ball more easily.

St. Aaron's Chapel.

Eventail Beach.

By that time, I was already suffering from asthma and this prevented me from running too far to fetch the ball which occasionally disappeared among the rocks or stagnant pools, and sometimes rolled into the sea whose presence, despite its immensity, we had quite forgotten.

On Sundays, my parents attended Mass in Rocabey, in Notre-Dame-des-Grèves, where once the sea had covered the land. I had to attend the school Mass. Then, beneath the huge glass roof in the assembly hall, there was the ceremonial reading out of the results of the weekly class tests. I can still remember as if it were yesterday the name of the pupil who, every Sunday for years on end, was always first in every subject - André Saint-Mieux. I saw him again later, successfully fulfilling each of his prestigious functions.

In fine weather, our parents would take us for drives through the countryside around Saint-Malo. We discovered superb beauty spots along the shores of the R. Rance, in Dol, Combourg, Cancale, Rothéneuf or Mont Saint-Michel which we knew by heart.

There were also brief visits to the paternal or maternal families, often for christenings, weddings or funerals. I enjoyed these visits, however short. They strengthened my understanding of my origins, a hamlet in the Deux-Sèvres, amidst the numerous members of the Gélin tribe, in rooms with beaten earth floors, near farmyards filled with the smells of rich mulch and animals, in which cousins chatted in local dialect while disposing of vast mountains of food during meals that were as generous as they were unpretentious. On occasions such as this, I had the soul of a long line of countrymen that were probably of Moorish origin, settling there after the Battle of Poitiers. Sometimes, we were in the heart of the Armor with the Le Meners, in an inn on the banks of the Nantes-Brest Canal. There, the cousins spoke Breton or a French pronounced with a tonic accent. The meals seemed interminable but they were an opportunity for sensitive, and hilarious, form of enjoyment. There, I felt I had the soul of the true Celt, full of feverish excitement and contrasting views.

In just a few years, my father enlarged his clientele. After the flat overlooking the Place de la Fontaine, we were fortunate enough to be able to occupy a large, comfortable villa on the Avenue Pasteur. In some ways, I was sorry to leave the Place de la Fontaine because, as I have said, the view from the windows was nothing short of sublime. I could watch high, stormy tides; immense columns of water, raised up by the fury of the surplus water and beaten down by the wind,

June 1933.

crashed against the Sillon, the promenade. I remember one storm when my mother forgot to close the double-glazed window of her bedroom. My parents' bed was soaked by the spuming crest of a salt-laden wave.

The roadway is wide. So is the pavement overlooking the sea, backed by a long wall. Despite this, on stormy days, the yard which, in those days, contained the house and was separated from it by a gateway some 10 ft. high, was found, on one occasion to have acquired a length of groyne that had been ripped up from the beach.

This was how I learnt that, in days gone by, the sea was not stopped in its tracks by the Sillon promenade. The Sillon used to consist of dunes which were reinforced by this granite causeway, but it was breached in several places to provide additional security for the walled town.

Saint-Malo really was an island, standing firm against the breakers to the north and west, letting the gentler waves lap the southern and eastern sides from Saint-Servan to the shores of Chasles, the marshy Rocabey and its dunes.

To get to l'Islet, people used flat-bottomed boats or, more frequently at low tide, horse-drawn carts. The tiny island provided a home for sedentary merchants, monks and crews awaiting their next passage. It was the seafarers who indulged in excesses. In his work, "Les Travailleurs de la Mer", Victor Hugo describes a veritable maritime underworld. And for many hundreds of years, terrifying bull mastiffs were used in the town to maintain law and order.

In our new home, life was very different. This was a fine building with a wrought-iron gate and a flight of steps leading into a hallway dominated by a vast staircase. Behind the house was a garden of modest size, which provided my mother with vegetables and flowers. In the spacious ground floor at our disposal, my sister and I set up an improvised theatre in which we performed short sketches and even plays during the school holidays. This was also a popular pastime on rainy days. For the acting "bug" had already begun to attack me.

When night fell, I began to live another existence altogether. I could only work and read in the late hours, when I felt more receptive, my brain less cluttered with other thoughts. Sometimes, I would wait until the household was asleep so that I could put my ear close up to the old Pathe-Marconi radio set and listen to dramas staged by the Rennes-Brittany theatre group. I used to turn the sound down so that I did not wake anybody up and listen to the play and the actors, all of whom I thought wonderful.

Despite the lack of sleep, I was never tired in the morning when I caught the school tramway, filled to overflowing with boys and girls who all made the sign of the

July 1933.

A stormy day
in Rochebonne.

Cross as they passed the great statue of the Crucifixion. The tramway stopped at the Rocabey crossroads where the wind was sometimes so strong that the trolleys were blown off the cables and where the storm was sometimes so violent that the Sillon was impassible. The furious, lashing sea had beaten its way into the Duguay-Trouin Basin and we had to make a detour via Saint-Servan in order to get to Saint-Malo, which had become an island again, as it had been in days gone by. An enormous, joyful sense of panic would stir our young blood, and the priests would forget their sternness for a time.

The main beach and the Hoguette Jetty.

The pupils from Dinard, despite having crossed the Rance Estuary amidst the rolling and pitching of the waves braved by the green and white motor launches would nevertheless have arrived in school before us. How invigorating and exciting we thought the violence of the sea whose very existence we sometimes forgot, so used were we to its presence!

In fact, I have remained as full of contrasts as the place and historical period which fashioned me. There is the excess and delirium of the sea (the evil of the storms and the call to travel, stopping in colourful ports full of exotic sights and dangers), and solitary meditation amidst the tranquillity of the beach at low tide, thoughts on the meaning of the cosmos which I used to indulge in as I gazed at the setting sun from the dyke, deserting the house, finding the spot where I still enjoy letting my thoughts wander.

As far as my decision to become an actor is concerned, I must tell you about the place where it probably took shape. It was a cinema, then known as the Emeraude-Palace, now called the Amiral. It stood right in the centre of the Sillon overlooking the sea. I often stopped there when I went into town, and I remained in the foyer, looking at the stills from the films that were being shown. By a happy chance, the managers of the cinema became close friends of my parents. The owner-projectionist was fond of me. He noticed my enthusiastic interest and often allowed me to watch the films from the projection room, through the tiny window from which I could see the screen, a magical sight with its white surface outlined in black. These were the days of the early talkies and magnetic sound tracks did not yet exist. The sound was recorded on an enormous black disk and I used to admire my friend's skill as he dropped the needle in place just as the first frame came on the screen. At that time, I saw a few melodramas that I have never forgotten, as well as the fashionable musical comedies. As cinema manager, the owner received all the magazines reserved for professionals and they taught me all the technical secrets, and kept me informed of projects and summaries of scripts. I read documents, and knew everything there was to know about the cinema since its infancy - L'Herbier, Abel Gance, Delluc, Charlie Chaplin, Harold Lloyd, Buster Keaton etc.

Sometimes, when it was raining, I was allowed to go and sit in the auditorium. I remember the first version of Ben Hur (with the wonderful music by Liszt). I was also very taken by Treasure Island, Captain Courageous, and L'Appel du silence.

As the years went by, I was given more freedom to come and go, and I would travel this way and that through the town and the surrounding area on my bicycle.

Place Chateaubriand.

43

After a brief period in the Sea Scouts (an organisation which was wound up because it was considered too dangerous), I enrolled in the Scout Troop in Paramé. Despite my lack of energy and my dislike of authority, I have touching memories of this experience. I could draw and paint fairly well and this flair for decoration won my patrol the first prize in a competition involving the whole of France. All this, taken with my tendency to dream and show a lack of emotion, resulted in my being given the troop nickname "Decorative lizard".

I used to love the hikes in the wild, untamed countryside nearby.

My love of entertainment, which resulted in my leading the campfires, won me a badge for being so full of fun. I also used to enjoy the few moments that followed the campfires proper, when we would sing a few old sea shanties. Then there would come the silence as the last embers died, lighting our young faces to the end, and the ritual, almost inaudible, murmur addressed to every member of the troop before we disappeared into our tents, "Good night, little brother! Good night, little brother!" which we would whisper in the chill of nightfall.

The camps were held during the school holidays, whatever the season. My two best-loved memories of them are still crystal clear in my mind.

First there was a Whitsun camp when, having escaped from continuous questioning, I felt in a mood to share my humour and communicative happiness, doubling my friends up with laughter and preventing the leaders from being too stern, even the Dominican almoner. We had set up our tents in a field sloping down to the dazzling, majestic River Rance. Between two bouts of acting the camp jester and the mandatory games, I succeeded in finding time for myself and I would set off to gaze at the shoreline along this long arm of the sea. The Dominican later admitted that he had been completely dumbfounded by these two extremes of my character - and he was to become more and more confused as time went on!

Then there was a Midnight Mass which I wanted to turn into an outstanding event. I succeeded in convincing the leaders to attend Mass, with all the rest of the troop, in Mont Saint-Michel, in the half-Romanesque, half-Gothic church whose parvis and esplanade overlook the entire bay. Darkness prevented us from seeing the waves or the shore, but in the chill, sacred atmosphere, after the Christmas hymns sung in Latin had filled and echoed round the vaulted roof, we could hear the cries and whirling flight of the seagulls aroused from their slumbers.

The years passed, with widely-differing activities filling the days depending on the season. In summer, we enjoyed ourselves on the beach, having uncomplicated fun.

July 1933.

Bon-Secours Beach.

**Môle Beach. In the distance
is the Bas-Sablons Harbour and the town of Alet.**

We could play tennis on the sand, for instance; it was quite hard enough. I can even remember an air show, held there because the available space and the quality of the ground was adequate for that purpose. In fact, there were almost always events to delight the sedentary population of Saint-Malo and amuse the summer holidaymakers who came in large numbers, year after year, drawn back here again and again by the charm of the town and the immense stretch of beach. Many families met up every year, after the 14th July. Some lodged in the fine villas that stood along the causeway; others in guest houses where they had become regular visitors. Spectacular regatas were held in the estuary, off Dinard. The main stands were set up on the breakwater that curved elegantly seawards, protecting the fishing boats tied up opposite the Dinan Gate.

It was here, on thick floating pontoons, that the Dinard ferries had their landing stages. And in Dinard the atmosphere was much more "select", with an upper-class clientele that included many British people.

Sometimes, I was able to see warships tied up in the harbour. Their presence was due solely to the fact that one of the town's M.P's had become Minister of the Navy! It was a custom that was to last for a few years.

Later, there were other warships tied up alongside. With their clean, dashing appearance, the might of their metal, and the efficiency of their machinery, I could not but think of war and its tragedies.

The future was to show how right I was.

In Saint-Malo, a few years later, friends often went to admire the ship captained by Admiral Darlan. I saw him on many occasions, dressed in civvies, in the local shops where he had a debonair appearance despite his regular, hard features. He was spoken of locally with a strange feeling of admiration, anxiety and perplexity. But that is quite another story.

I often went to look at the Pourquoi-Pas, usually when it was tied up along the quay, a graceless, massive, heavily-built vessel. Commandat Charcot was already a legendary figure by that time. I looked enviously at the sailors daydreaming on the deck. All of them were young, and all seemed to exude a sense of adventure. I may even have been looking at one of the sailors whom I met years later, Paul-Emile Victor. It was he who came up and spoke to me one day on the quayside in Saint-Tropez, giving me a warm handshake. Having just returned from one of his first expeditions, he had seen Rendez-vous de Juillet, a film in which I playd a young explorer. We became friends, seeing each other from time to time, in many different

Bon-Secours Beach.

corners of the globe. Together, we would chat about adventure, and I can still hear him telling me about the adventures of the legendary Commandant Charcot and his ship, the "Pourquoi-Pas?" which had given me so much to dream about when she put in to Saint-Malo.

At school, my success was no more than average. My abysmal lack of mathematical knowledge could not be compensated for by my imagination in the French class! Being naturally undisciplined and rowdy, and being given to a habit of lazily daydreaming, I was the despair of my father who had cherished ideas of my taking over from him. He would also have been delighted if I had become the captain of a trawler. Certain ships' captains, who were much sought after for their shrewdness and skill, were paid on a commission basis. They had enviable jobs and were greatly admired. In those days, many of these great sailors had begun life in modest circumstances and had learnt their art on the "Banks". Let loose in pairs in dories, they fished with rods, sometimes sailing dangerously far away from the sailing ship lost in the ice-laden fog. Some of them had attended the Hydrography College to which my father hoped to send me. I had nothing against the idea but I did not seem to be heading in that direction. Despite a still fervent faith, I was becoming increasingly interested in the town's fairer sex, often my sister's friends. My sister, on the other hand, was gifted as regards studying. Her school was in the old walled town at the end of the Place des Jardins-de-l'Evêché beyond the cathedral. The two schools shared an English teacher. Taking advantage of a moment's inattention, which was easy, we used to slide billets doux for the schoolgirls beneath the leather band round his hat. The girls would answer in the same way. We were delighted to think that he walked right through the town, passing the cathedral as he went, and obsequiously greeting some of the local people who were the parents of his pupils, carrying our love letters with him!

Because of my undisciplined nature and given the fact that I was going to have to repeat a year, my parents decided to quell me by registering me as a boarder. Life became austere. We used to rise at 5.30 every morning for communion. My fury and reputation were such that I was watched particularly closely by a perfectly odious housemaster who terrorised the entire school and whom no pupil who has ever attended the school in Saint-Malo can forget (Xavier Grall still talked about him to me many years later). He was a priest and was partly responsible for my gradual dislike of the Roman Catholic church, yet he proved to be a veritable hero during the fire in the summer of 1944.

I am first on the right in the third row.

The spire of the cathedral.

48

My first communion.

The only benefit I gained from being a boarder was the conviction that there must be some way of bringing the teaching of Christianity into line with greater knowledge of the Bible, a feature which was completely ignored in the school where much greater importance was placed on the learning of the liturgies. It was a strange, archaic institution in which the philosophy of the great man of St-Malo, Lamennais, still seemed to be rejected. I discovered it much, much later. In addition to this revelation, I was delighted to belong to the choir which often sung in the cathedral itself. With its cloying dimness, the cathedral in which all the great navigators had come to pray and which was situated at the bottom of a slope before the war, resembled a vast, austere crypt full of humidity and much-suited to meditation. But the choir, placed high up, in which my soprano voice expressed a deep-seated fervour, brought me a sense of freedom and I knew, even at that time, that whichever path my faith was to take in later years, I would retain a love of sacred song to my last breath (1).

My parents decided to free me from the strain of being a boarder. I became an average pupil again, and much better-behaved for being less unhappy.

It was at this time that I gained a wonderful friend, Xavier, whom I shall never forget. He had arrived only a short time before from Paris, from a fashionable literary and aristic milieu, and he was very different to my other friends. He did not belong to any clique or group. He was intelligent, eccentric, full of humour and poetry, lucid yet a dreamer, in short a being from another world.

We got on perfectly together. After coming home from school, usually along the beach, he would do his homework in my house and learn the lessons for the following day before going home. His father lived in Rothéneuf, in an isolated house in the midst of the fields, a large stocky building with a sturdy tower to one side that was reminiscent of Montaigne's house. It was known as "Windy Tower". This man, who was of such importance in my life, was called Théophile Briant. After having been an integral part of the Paris that had become aware of art in the 1920's, he had owned several galleries in which he had exhibited works by Monet, Max Jacob, Rouault, Utrillo, Vlaminck, Gauguin and Picasso, among others. One day, like Saint-Pol-Roux, he had been overwhelmed by solitude and had come to settle in "Windy Tower", not far from the cliffs of Paramé. Colette, who stayed in the area from 1911 to 1924, wrote Le Blé en herbe there before her "Treille muscate" in Saint-Tropez and was, with so many other lovers of the sea and beauty, one of Théo's close friends.

The chancel in the cathedral.

50

From time to time, as we heard through Xavier, he would take a trip up to Paris and meet his friends at Lipp's.

Of the poetic and artistic activity, we heard only vague details but it was all shrouded in mysteries that, strangely enough, attracted me. When I cycled to Rothéneuf and the wind from the sea buffeted me from the left, I could see, high above the landscape, the famous "Windy Tower" that seemed to me to contain all sorts of magic spells. I was one of the few who were privileged to enter the house.

In it was a vast room filled to overflowing with books, signed photographs, unexpected objects and eloquent remains which gave me an impression of entering the sanctuary of a rather mystical alchemist flirting with the mysterious. Nor was I mistaken. The master of the house's delight in Villiers de l'Isle-Adam, Barbey d'Aurevilly, Rimbaud, Nerval, Milosh and Corbière impregnated the atmosphere in the house. A small bedroom on the ground floor was the haunt of my friend, Xavier. His father had a round rubicond face, dazzling smile, and picturesque turn of speech. He also had an aura of immense goodness and a real presence. This marginality, which nevertheless bore the imprint of Christian faith, seemed to disturb the teachers somewhat. In fact, I am convinced that some of them must have read Le Goëland, the poetry and art magazine that Théophile Briant launched on 22nd June 1936 at the summer equinox, which included philosophical and poetic chronicles. Much was said about magic and the occult in this revue and among the poets published for the first time and encouraged in its pages were René-Guy Cadou, Anne de Tourville, Patrice de La Tour du Pin, Luc Bérimont, Charles Le Quintrec and Louis le Cunff (1).

One day, towards the end of the winter during a school holiday period, I was stricken by a piece of news, the first dramatic event to overtake any of my friends. While his parents were away in Paris, Xavier had accidentally killed himself in "Windy Tower" while playing with a friend. He had been amusing himself by firing a revolver at the seagulls and, when showing off the principle of the safety catch to his friend, had made a fatal error and shot himself through the heart. He did not die immediately. A priest was rushed to the scene and Xavier took care to ensure that his friend was not left to bear any responsibility for the accident. At once, with my friend Robert Rodas, I went to "Windy Tower". I shall never forget his parents' sadness. His mother, white-faced and drawn, sat alone in a corner, in the darkness. Théo welcomed us and took us into Xavier's small bedroom. Our friend lay on his bed, cadaverous, dressed in the school uniform that so resembled the uniform of naval officers, his hands clasped on a Crucifix. Théo could not tear

(1) In the last four volumes of Robert Sabatier's work, *L'Histoire et la Poésie*, which deal with the 20th century, Théophile Briant is quoted frequently.

his eyes away from the scene and kept repeating the same words, over and over again, "little man, my little man". A few days later, the hearse, weighed down by bouquets and wreaths of white flowers, took our young playmate to the modest St. Ideuc's Church and from there to the tiny cemetery. It was a country road, through the fields. The entire school followed, with the friends and relations who had come from Paris. It was raining, just as it rained during the funeral of Daudet's character, Petit Chose. "My, how it rained!"

I learned that Xavier's mother had lost her reason. For years, Théo had to employ a nun from a nursing Order, but he continued to live in his now-accursed house, writing and editing his revue, Le Goëland. In a sort of ritual and dialogue with the elements, he would swim every day, whatever the season and whatever the weather. He only had to cross the road and go down the dunes before pitting himself against the sea.

My own sense of sorrow and loss was enormous. Out or fear or respect, I did not have the courage to go and see Théo for several years. I knew that my father and he often saw each other on the causeway and that they raised their hats to each other without ever daring to speak. It was not until much later, when I was making a film with Lucien Baroux (a great film star and a close friend of Théo's since their days together in the First World War trenches) that I saw Théo coming to see him on the set. He looked at me as if he had lost the power of speech.

Théo Briant.

I was by then more than twenty years old and I was filming, as an equal, with his best friend. Xavier would have been the same age as me... He murmured to himself, "It's young Gélin!" and hugged me to his chest.

I have already said that Le Goëland was first published in 1936. This was also, as we know, the year in which the Popular Front introduced paid holidays for workers. My mother, who was a devout Catholic, burst into tears when she heard Léon Blum stating, on the radio, that "The government of the Popular Front has been duly constituted" for she feared, quite wrongly, that there might be a few excesses among these members of the lay population. My father, who was wiser and more lucid, tried to reassure her. As far as I was concerned, there were few changes in my life at school. The government had made sports mandatory every Saturday afternoon. The priests sagely applied the law and we were forced to attend the sports ground. Gradually, the fathers relaxed their supervision until their strict discipline failed to such an extent that we were able to "skip" sport without any risks. Several of us took advantage of these afternoons off to go to Dinard on the green and white launches, braving the swell to go to the luxurious villa deserted by the parents of a

pupil from Paris who entertained us. We were accompanied by a few attractive teenage girls, all of them dazzling and precocious as they tend to be sometimes in harbour towns. Jazz music blared out. These were my first "parties". And I must thank Léon Blum and the relaxed discipline of our teachers who enabled us to begin and perfect a type of education that they had not foreseen!

In the summer, larger crowds of holidaymakers came to the beaches, especially Parisians. Their sons showed a rather untimely tendency to sneer and display their bravado but they had no success with the girls, from our home town or from anywhere else, for the young ladies showed deeper understanding and our manners, which were never rustic but were more romantic, delighted them much more easily.

It is time for me to tell of an incident that strengthened me very early on in my resolve. For a few years, within the walled town, there had been a number of grill

A hydrofoil arriving from the Channel Islands in Saint-Malo.

room/cafes that had had the idea of showing high-quality films during the summer months, projected onto screens fitted up facing their terraces and, in some places, projected directly onto the ramparts themselves. At nightfall, we would take our folding stools and go to see all the box office successes of the silent era followed, a few years later, by the talkies. What a miracle! There was no discordant jangle of sounds! And if, from a distance, another film looked more interesting, we merely had to move our stools along and change terraces. This phenomenon lasted for several summers. In the winter, we would frequent the church halls where we could enjoy the forerunners of the film clubs of a later era. I am convinced that this uninterrupted love of the cinema, which was satisfied on Vauban's ramparts and in the small, emotionally moving halls of Paramé, Saint-Malo and Saint-Servan was instrumental in my determination to become an actor.

The carved rocks in Rothéneuf. In the distance is the Bigne.

The Privateers' Town huddling round the cathedral, as seen from the main beach.

T★★★★★★★ he devil had caught hold of me and, at school in winter, I was more undisciplined and less attentive than ever. I was a frequent visitor "at the pillory", the place where prisoners and criminals were once put on public ★★★★★★★ view. It was at the top of the Rue Saint-Vincent and it was here that the town's teenagers congregated. Personally, I made no attempt to rival peers with greater physical attributes; instead, I cultivated a more discreet romanticism which often took me away from the group with a young girl from Saint-Malo to corners along the walls or in the Holland Bastion gardens. When darkness fell, and it fell quickly, we were able to lie down on a raincoat spread out on the sands on Bon-Secours Beach. It was all the more romantic and poetic because the beams from the lighthouses opposite (in the Garden and on the Breakwater) not only guided unsure cargo boats into harbour from the open sea; they also swept furtively across the beach, briefly lighting up our romantic, but nevertheless impatient, love affairs.

My schoolwork became more and more disappointing. When I was in the Fourth Form, a teacher who, in my opinion, showed unjust favouritisim to a few children from good families, was treated after a lesson and during a break of which I had been deprived to the ultimate French swear word. I had been biting it back for months and it burst out with a force and a sense of joyous liberation that echoed round the vast empty study room! I was expelled on the spot. My father immediately took me on in his docks as an assistant warehouseman and I got to know the atmosphere that reigns along the wharves of the Duguay-Trouin Basin. I had to work hard, learning and trying my hand at splicing and whipping before cutting the hemp or steel cables. I had to cut off lengths of sailcloth, and, on many occasions, deliver bales of sisal on board ship. My father paid me and I bought books which I devoured at night, writers such as Maurois, Dickens, Hugo and Roger Vercel. I had a particular liking for Saint-Exupéry, Kessel and Musset (La Confession d'un Enfant du siècle).

In order to reward me for my efforts, my father tried to find me a job in the office but I turned out to be useless. I made mistakes in schedules and did not give the correct change.

I returned to my job as assistant-warehouseman. While reading the cinema magazine called Ciné-Monde, I learned that there was a drama school in Paris which prepared young hopefuls for a career in the theatre and cinema - it was the Cours René Simon. One day, while my father was on board a ship, I ran over to the post office in Rocabey and phoned the school. René Simon, who had no idea I was *phoning from the provinces, said shortly, "I see potential new students on Tuesdays" and hung up.*

Leaving provincial life at the age of seventeen in those pre-war years, when one belonged to a practising Catholic family filled with simple prejudices and ignorant of all but a few towns in Western France and its deeply rural areas, to become part of a social set in which, as everybody knows, life is nothing but debauchery, vice and mortal sin, was a challenge on my part, and a nameless form of audacity. I knew this very well but I was staunchly determined to shake off the middle class life that was stifling me. More importantly, I felt the need to create the real me and would let nothing stand in the way of what I felt was a vocation. There are those who may have considered this decision to be based largely on naivety and innocence but I believe that the same innocence and thoughtlessness must have fired all those who set out on any form of adventure. I was certainly inspired by the example set by a number of figures from Saint-Malo.

So, here I was in Paris; it was 1st April 1939. René Simon, who was initially startled by my juvenile appearance, gave me an audition and agreed to enroll me in his class until the summer.

During these three months, I discovered a fascinating city and a world that I had never suspected - the theatre. The students in the class sometimes seemed to me to be rather superficial. But there were others who were, fortunately, enthusiastic and I already shared with them an almost priestlike feeling for the acting profession. I worked hard with a great deal of fervour and I attended plays as a future participant rather than with the sensitivity of a mere member of the audience.

Tarzan !!!

In the summer, I returned to Saint-Malo and the new family home that my father had had built in the Avenue Pasteur. My sister had become very beautiful and had begun studying medicine in Rennes. My parents seemed to be pleased with their offspring. My enthusiastic comments on the art of being an actor reassured my father. We were thoughtless, despite the parades of Hitlerian armies shown on the cinema newsreels! Mussolini's histrionics made us merely shrug our shoulders. Personally, I had no opinions about leading French politicians. The constant changeover of government ministers and portfolios had long since left us blase. I lost myself in books and fell in love with a stunning young girl named Nicole, the daughter of a barrister from Strasburg. She was the only one to speak anxiously about the threat of war and

59

its consequences. She had very long hair, a wonderful body and huge eyes. She talked to me about the rumours that had spread from Germany; she said she was frightened and that she was afraid for her family. She was a Jew.

The summer was magnificent. With my friends, we did a lot of sailing. We went to the Conchée Fort, then to Cézembre. From this distance offshore, we could see the Privateers' Town in the dusk. Lit up by the sun that was soon to sink below the horizon in the west, it seemed to have an unreal beauty. Its belltower, rising from the very centre of the town, looked very different to the ship's mast to which it had so often been compared. The steeple, a traceried edifice at that time, had an elegance and a grace that, instead of contrasting with the massive heaviness of the ramparts, seemed on the contrary to give practical expression to all the architectural forms of the town. It erased the fortress-like appearance of the town as a whole, an appearance that had already been dimmed by the tall slate roofs, and stood like a homage to all that heaven held sacred, a challenge to the threats of the deep.

All these boat trips, which we had already undertaken during our adolescence, increased our admiration for our town, and our passionate reverence increased with age as we acquired greater sensitivity. Seen from the sea, Saint-Malo is a set of impressions, and a series of surprises that everybody should have a chance to discover. On the return journey, the closer we moved to the town, the more it seemed to rise up out of the waves, swelling in size. These feelings were heightened by the skilful manoevering that was required if we were to avoid the reefs and escape the numerous, versatile currents in the estuary.

Personally, having already seen something of Paris and its very different atmosphere, I may perhaps have had a heightened appreciation of the beauty through which we were sailing. Beyond the breakwater, we were surrounded by a sense of quiet tranquillity, but the drunken sensations of the open sea in our small sailing boats still filled our blood and mind, with even greater serenity. After crossing the town and passing through the Dinan Gate, we would finish the day in the Bar de l'Univers on the Place Chateaubriand, the haunt of all the great seadogs who were so well illustrated by Marin Marie.

We were thoughtless, as I said. We liked jazz. There were parties galore and they were times of senseless merriment. All of us were in tune with the gentle frivolity and youth expressed in Charles Trenet's song, "Je chante!". We seemed to have taken an enchanted pathway. Here, as everywhere else in France during that summer, we were singing and dancing on a volcano!

The town walls seen from the Holland Bastion,
with the Naye Slipway in the background.

When we were not going for long cycle rides that took us to the beaches at La Guimorais, Le Rocher in Cancale and, more particularly, the Pointe du Grouin which, for me, has remained unrivalled as a spot in which to meditate, we simply stayed on the main beach, usually on the most sheltered part stretching along the front of the Grand Hotel in Paramé.

I used to read a lot, late into the night, and even on the beach. I hired from the local library the entire bound collection of Petite Illustration which included all the plays created since I was born. I read them all. But I did not dare to give back the huge album; its pages gaped as a result of the silent infiltration of fine sand.

Then came the announcement that we were at war. The news broke like a clap of distant thunder. Disbelievingly we lived through it as it were no more than a nightmare. A feeling common to great moments in History. Yet, deep inside, we felt that the history of the world, or at least the history of Europe, was about to topple over and this vague awareness, in which fear played no part, set my head spinning. Unlike all my friends, who quickly became given to nationalistic sentiment and jingoism with a degree of warlike glorification, my feelings underwent constant change. Firstly, I felt angry with politics and the politicians who had been so irresponsible; then I felt profound desolation at the terrible absurdity of it all. Among these vague sensations, there was only one certainty - our town had never been conquered. At least we could be reassured about that. After all, our M.P. was Minister of the Air Force and he had declared that the French Air Force was invincible! Be that as it may, there was no question of my returning to Paris and I was already dreading my return to the docks in the Duguay-Trouin Basin. My fine dreams lay in shreds. But I then received a letter from René Simon telling me that, despite the war, the show must go on and that he was relying on me. He also added that some of the students at the National Drama College had been called up and that I could therefore enroll. I had a chance of passing the examinations.

As I write these details, I am reminded of a scene from Entrée des Artistes by Marc Allégret. I had seen the film projected on the town walls, with Louis Jouvet in his own role as the teacher, and all the young student actors whom I had so desperately wanted to join.

I travelled back to Paris and, a few weeks later, found myself in that very class!

My cultural knowledge was expanding; so was my conception of art. I realised this each time I returned to Saint-Malo where, in addition to the joy of rediscovering the

A stroll along the walls and Bon-Secours Beach.

62

The town walls and shipowners' houses seen from the castle.

balance of family life and the feverish excitement of my first love affairs, my solitary walks created in me a thirst for adventure that was stronger than the thirsts quenched in any sailors' bars, whatever the type. I also felt a call to a love of others that had to be expressed and communicated, to a deeper knowledge of what is known as the spiritual. It is obvious that the much-loved town with which I felt at one was strengthening an inherent sense of harmony.

Saint-Malo, the granite town, the cradle of heroes in every field, is also a Muse who has to be won over.

During one of my trips back home, I don't remember the exact date, I saw regiments of the British Army marching along the road in front of the villa; they had landed that very morning. A few days later, it was the turn of the Canadians, stirred by the thought that they were in Saint-Malo from which their ancestors had set out for the New World. My emotion was at its height. They set off for the hill at Paramé where convoys of lorries were to take them to the Front. And they were scarcely any older than I was! The "phony war" had begun.

In the capital, we were conditioned by our studies, and completely engrossed in our own world, a universe in which only the expression of art and culture had any meaning. The rumblings of war seemed to us to be distant and muffled.

Suddenly, the news became more believable. It was said that the Wehrmacht was invading France. That spring was one of the most humiliating I have ever experienced. Paris quickly became deserted. I don't know what made me stay. The weather was hot. Passers-by walked slowly, their resignation obvious. Cocteau made up a spoonerism, which was a wonderfully apt description of the last remaining Parisians walking aimlessly as if world-weary, "A Paris, les gens circulent dans leur chaise à torpeur" (In Paris, people loiter in their litters). Finally, I set off for Saint-Malo where the beauty of the sunshine seemed to clash with the atmosphere of shame and mortification.

Saint-Malo did not appear to be suffering the general feelings of consternation that had led most of France to set off on a disastrous exodus. It was because the sea was present, terribly present, and the town that Man had built remained as steadfast as ever. I found that a few people had left the town and that all the friends of my age had cycled off to Bordeaux. Moreover, devoid of its summer holidaymakers, the whole town with its empty, crowdless beaches seemed beautiful in my eyes; it seemed to have gained greater nobility. The locals were a people full of courage and wisdom. My parents were desperately sorry for what had happened, and thoroughly ashamed. The harbour traffic ebbed.

The National Fort seen from the Bidouane Tower.

Nicole had become permanently based in Saint-Malo. We did our utmost to ignore her fear for her loved ones, her parents' rage, the stagnant misfortune that could be felt in the air and in homes. June had never been so beautiful. It seemed as if the entire world and its terrible misunderstandings had agreed to let our love blossom. All the beaches were ours for the taking. We took refuge in even more secretive corners, on beaches elsewhere along the coast where the emerald green sea, the lapping waves and the fabulous caves brought to our world all the serenity of the shores of Polynesia.

One day, towards evening, we heard that the Germans had arrived. Quickly we cycled to the barracks in Rocabey where, indeed, we saw the Volkswagens of elegant

The National Fort at high tide seen from the Eventail Slipway.

young officers driving through the gates, their faces filled with a tranquillity that owed nothing to arrogance.

My companion could not contain her anger and fear when she saw the Hitlerian swastika flying over the barracks. Yet it was all steeped in a sense of unreality.

We decided to continue our disdainful rejection of events. Our friends, who later returned from their flight to Bordeaux, harrassed, had agreed to ignore the presence of the occupying forces whose soldiers occasionally wandered through the streets of the old town, their boots ringing out hesitantly on the cobbles.

The temperature soared to abnormal heights throughout the summer. For a few evenings, the phenomenon brought millions of sardines and mackerel close in to the shore and we went fishing in Paramé as the tide rose, among the rocks just in front of us. When the banks of mackerel met the banks of sardines, there was a splashing and seething beneath the surface. The massacre was ferocious; the clash of scales was dazzling. Balanced on the rocks, were some one hundred or more young lads from Saint-Malo, casting their lines. All that was needed as bait were a few sardines, still streaming with water but caught in a corner from which they could not escape. Thanks to them, we took home huge quantities of greedy mackerel. This event was unique in the whole of Saint-Malo's history. Yet to the few flabbergasted Jerries we met, we declared shortly, tranquilly and in a vaguely blasé tone that here in Saint-Malo this was a frequent, nay very common, occurence!

In an effort to show even less awareness of their presence in our town, for a few convalescent soliders had taken over the bedrooms and beach of the Grand Hotel, we decided to go camping on a wild island in the middle of the R. Rance known as Dog's Island. We camped in magnificent tents that the British Army had left behind in its rush when it was ignobly re-embarking for its dear England! We spent a few, exquisite weeks on the island. We ate the fish we caught and the ormers that a few of our friends, swimming without masks, would slice off the surrounding rocks nine or ten feet beneath the surface of the waves. A few of us rowed across to a village on the shore to buy the necessary items of food. I remember the strength of the current. We had to pull hard on the oars. One day, when we landing on the other shore, a few Jerries, who were probably drunk at the time, began to take pot shots at us. We sought refuge behind the rocks on the shore. The bullets whistled around us, splattering into the granite, and it was a miracle that none of us was hit. Apart from this one incident, we were unnaturally happy. Most of the members of our band were former Scouts and we were perfectly capable of organising our leisure

1941, the Dinan Slipway. St-Malo fishermen and German soldiers at the landing stage for the green launches.

activities. Discussions carried on late into the night around the campfire. I remember having taken advantage of the sense of meditation and filled the silence broken only by the wide, soothing murmur of the waves by reciting a few poems by Baudelaire and Rimbaud.

My days, which were still filled with a basic unawareness of what was going on, became even more intense when a few sentimental fiancees with fire in their veins, moved by the isolation of the spot and the veiled ambiguity of the drama that was spoiling our youth and blinding us to any future, came to join us on an island that was forgotten by the rest of the world.

Alas! There came a day when we had to return to terra firma and all that it had in store for us in the way of mishaps and misfortunes.

At the end of the summer of 1940, I returned to Paris. There I started studying at the Conservatoire (the equivalent of RADA) under Mrs. Dussane, since Jouvet had fled to South America. That very day, I was given my first role in the theatre, at Le Grand Guignol in a play by Clouzot directed by Pierre Fresnay who, in the absence of Jouvet, became a fatherly adviser, full of warmth and lucidity. My visits to Saint-Malo became increasingly rare. My bedroom and my sister's room were both occupied by German soldiers who worked in the bunkers and other major installations belonging to the Todt Organisation, in Alet.

But it was written that Saint-Malo was to be the scene of important changes in my life.

One day, late in the afternoon when the tide was low, I was alone, not far from "Windy Tower", in a deserted meadow in which the grass shivered in the freshness of the air. I was lying on my back, looking up at a deep blue, cloudless sky that stretched into infinity when suddenly I was struck by a physical sensation of emptiness, of desertion on a major scale. He was no longer there, I was sure of it. I could not feel His presence any longer, He had abandoned me. Who? God, quite simply. I can say this without shame or false modesty. I had thought I could pray, live for Him and for His laws, fervently, lovingly, and He had abandoned me. I shall never forget this moment. I have never really recovered from it, and I am sure that the affliction could not have happened elsewhere, in Paris or in a faceless room. It had to happen outside, on this tall cliff overlooking the vast beach, murmuring at low tide, beneath the deep blue sky.

Often, now that I have finally reached the age of wisdom in which I can still feel the flutterings of a final form of adolescence but with balance sheets that cause the soul

My first Harcourt portrait, taken on my arrival in Paris in 1939.

less torment and meditations that are more tranquil, however ambitious the projects remain, I think long and hard of this moment.

How much easier it is for me to understand the thoughts of Lamennais and the immodest yet finally serene transes full of enchantment created by the style of Chateaubriand.

The months passed. Danièle Delorme had come into my life, forcefully and publicly. My sister, Monique, had come to be with me in Paris. We lived a bohemian life, full of harmonious disorder, tolerance, and poetry. My friends were different and sensitive; we had been thrown together by a wonderful opportunity. The Allied landings had finally taken place, after a multitude of rumours and uncertainties. My parents had sought refuge in Angers, since my mother had somewhat overindulged her interest in the messages transmitted from London by the radio, in the presence of Germans.

It was on my return from Haute-Marne with some very close friends that we rediscovered Paris with its joys, its excessive clearing-up operations, and its reunions, as well as its disappointments. We thought that Danièle's mother, who had been deported to Ravensbrück, would soon be home but this was not so. We had to wait many more, long months before we saw her again. One evening, we went to the Gaumont-Palace cinema on the Place Clichy, to see Charlie Chaplin in The Dictator. During the newsreel that preceded the film, I saw pictures that upset me deeply. The camera, having filmed the St. Vincent Gate intact, showed my town, a vast pile of smoking ruins, stretches of wall standing like ghosts, a relentless, astounding sight that made me burst uncontrollably into tears.

Versions differ with regard to details of the destruction. For a long time, I thought that only the Americans had bombed the town from Paramé, using incendiary bombs, but there was also German fire from the island of Cézembre. The four hundred people of Saint-Malo who had taken refuge in the National Fort watched as their town was set ablaze. It is known that the Germans demolished the steeple on the cathedral. Since that time, I have never known what to believe. Dr. Tuloup, in his masterly work, Histoire de Saint-Malo, (Saint-Malo in which he had done his duty amidst the inferno) is unable to be more precise.

Our town probably fell victim to crossfire and he is quite right to state that, "The guilty party was War itself. It is an archaic, barbarous, out-of-date solution, which 20th-century man, a race of over-intelligent scientists, still conjures up fearlessly".

The St. Vincent Gate.

****** *

A *few years later, in Hollywood, during the making of a film with Alfred Hitchcock, I was in James Stewart's house for a party that he had organised for those who knew and loved France. There I met an American director name Joshua Logan, who spoke French admirably well (he had translated the entire works of Pagnol). He asked me which town I came from in France. When I said Saint-Malo, I saw the great old man pale before saying with sincere sorrow in his voice, "I was an officer in the American batteries in Paramé and what you saw on the newsreel, I lived through. I went through the St. Vincent Gate myself". And before almost all Hollywood, tears streamed down his cheeks, unchecked.*

****** *

T *he reconstruction of the town was, and will always be, seen as a masterful enterprise. The well-established determination of the local architects, old quarrels forgotten, who combined their knowledge of the locality with the enthusiastic skill of the great Parisian architects and their modernity, was to result, thanks also to the resolve and conviction of Guy La Chambre, in the harmonious masterpiece that is the new Saint-Malo. The architects (and it is only right to mention Mr. Cornon, assisted by Louis Arretche and Marc de Laujardière) are worthy successors of Garangeau. The synthesis of "legendary physionomy" and subtle improvements is, in my mind, the only example of its kind anywhere in the world. It is difficult today to imagine how much enthusiasm and fury was required at the outset to clear away the heap of ruins, to remove remaining mines, set aside and number some of the stones. Before they could take up their obliterated seafaring activities again, the people of Saint-Malo had to empty the basins of an accumulation of wrecks, lying hard up against the boats that had foundered there. They had to repair the breakwater and the locks. As soon as the Germans had gone, the American engineers assisted them in clearing the entrance to the basins. In 1946, the Quai Duguay-Trouin was repaired and gradually maritime trade began to build up again, in a much-improved harbour. The privateers' walled town came out of the massacre grander and greater than before. All the people of Saint-Malo, indeed all Frenchmen, should be proud of it and feel stronger and more noble for its existence.*

The cathedral in ruins.

The main street and the cathedral.

70

The cour
La Houssaye

In 1946, I married Danièle Delorme. We spent the summer in Saint-Malo, in the house that my parents had just rebuilt. Our son, Xavier, became a happy, and familiar, sight on the beach not far from the villa in front of what was then the Grand Hôtel in Paramé (1). We used to walk him along the causeway in his pram. Although we were busy working and climbing the ladder in our profession, I wanted to show Danièle my town and my region. It was then that I took over an amateur dramatic company which had had its moment of glory before the war. It was known somewhat pompously as The Mountebanks of the Emerald Coast ("Les baladins de la Côte d'Emeraude"). Assisted by a master sailmaker, I painted the sets myself, in a vast corner of the docks run by my father, who was somewhat dazed to see me relinquishing an opportunity to laze on the beach and go swimming. Danièle and some friends volunteered to search for furniture in the antique shops in Paramé and the costumes were hired from the theatre in Rennes. We "advertised" in Ouest-France and, after one month's rehearsal, we set off by car to stage a series of one-act plays selected to suit the personalities of the amateur actors. The sets could all be dismantled, and they were tied onto the roofrack of my father's Peugeot. It was good fun and very exciting. Danièle played Jules Renard's Poil de Carotte again, the role which marked her real debut, in Cannes, during the war. I was obliged to play Father Lepic. Then we played Courteline. Our shows were staged in any villages that agreed to let us perform, in village halls or church halls, and even on a table tennis table. The "boxes" were in the chicken roosts! We were particularly successful in Dol-de-Bretagne, Saint-Suliac, Tinténiac, and on the other side of the R. Rance. I was surprised and delighted to meet a parish priest who had once taught the Fifth Form in the secondary school and who was subject to a certain amount of derision in the tiny village where he now worked. He lent us the barn. It was a brotherly, moving gesture.

That summer, without telling me her plans, Danièle knocked on the door of "Windy Tower", Théo's house, and showed him some of my poetry, in which he saw something of interest. He welcomed me warmly. We became frequent visitors to the house, which was still isolated in the middle of the fields and was still filled with the magical presence of scholarly tomes and works of real poetry. Théo spoke to us with his elegant eloquence and devotion of all that he knew, describing the great navigators and discoverers of continents, and the real poets who comforted him or whom he had been fortunate enough to bring to the attention of the public.

(1) Now the Hôtel des Thermes, a wonderful marine hydrotherapy centre to which I am a frequent visitor.

Boats sunk in the harbour.

One morning, Théo himself came to see me in the villa. He introduced me to a small, young woman who seemed almost possessed. She was blind, an unknown poetess, yet one day she had rushed up to "Windy Tower". "Sit down and listen to her," he said. There, in the middle of the family lounge, I saw and heard the vibrant voice of this young girl, a girl possessed, as she spoke words that were a homage to life, to God, to love, and to the most immodest form of sensuality. I reeled beneath the shock. Never again would I see this state of possession, except perhaps in Maria Casarès or Edith Piaf. This young blind girl was called Angèle Vannier. This was a summer of unusually intense emotions. Danièle and I were filled with hope. Of course, we were steeped in the town that was already, miraculously, beginning to rise from the ruins again. I met up with a few old friends in the Bar de l'Univers. And I shall never get over the disappointment of not having had time to accompany Klippfel in a trip to the Channel Islands, to which he sailed often, "come hell or high water". Despite my attraction for the sea, my love of the theatre was stronger, and my personal cabin boy was the woman who, in later years, was to become Colette's Gigi, Anouilh's Colombe, and Claudel's Violaine. We set off for Paris, promising we would come back again.

In the autumn, near Tours, my sister who had given up studying medicine married Marc Lauer, the manager of the Billancourt film studios and the producer of Remorques. It was Marc de Laujardière, the architect who had helped to design the rebuilding of Saint-Malo, who had introduced them to each other. He had written that the fate of the Gélin children was to be sealed with the family of the silver screen and the rebirth of their adopted town!

My mother died the following Christmas. Despite this, I played my role during the matinee and the evening performance of Cocteau's Parents terribles, a role that I had taken over from Jean Marais. In the play, the mother died on the stage and she, too, was called Yvonne, like my own mother. Torn with anguish when I heard the actor who was playing my father crying the name several times, I could not help imagining my own father at Dr. Ferey's clinic in Rothéneuf. The funeral was held in Notre-Dame-des-Grèves and the cemetery in Rocabey. The blue granite tombstone was designed by Marc de Laujardière.

The next few years saw me caught up in a whirlwind of professional engagements - cinema, theatre, and radio. Often I was to escape, and visit my father. Every summer, Xavier spent the holidays with his grandfather. Then, for a few years, as if seized by a burst of energy and a fear of a paralysing loneliness, it was my father who

In Angers with Théo Briant (on the left).

The Solidor Tower.

decided to undertake frequent visits to Paris. This was good for all of us. For me, it was a moving sight to see my father on the Champs-Elysées, on film sets, or even in Saint-Germain-des-Prés, strolling along and taking exercise, always wearing the navy blue felt "captain's" cap, that he had first adopted when he arrived Saint-Malo.

Despite the illness which he faced up to courageously and goodtemperedly, he continued his trips to the capital until the day he was forced to take to his bed.

In my turn, I went to visit him, as often as I was able. These brief visits to the walled town of Saint-Malo cleaned out the artificial aspects and petty triumphs of my profession. Moreover, I noticed that my father's health was declining at the same speed as the reconstruction of the town was progressing.

After our divorce, which was arranged without any sense of animosity, Danièle Delorme continued to come and see him, her generosity obvious to all.

When I returned from America, I introduced him to Sylvie, my second wife, who loved old people and was, in her turn, admirable with him. My father, who was seriously ill, had let himself go somewhat. It was not until he learned that Sylvie was expecting a child that, by a sort of obstinate determination, he miraculously rallied.

When his grandson, Pascal, was born, he let destiny follow its course - he considered that he had had his time. Have I any right to say of Death that, sometimes, it chooses its relentless dates "well"? A year later, after the almost serene departure of my father, I lost my son, Pascal. They were buried side by side in Rocabey. There were a lot of people at the funeral but I only remember Théo, his face altered beyond recognition by a sense of fatality.

Later, in one of his writings, I read the expression "father-orphan". His death followed, sudden and brutal, that same year, in a banal road accident. This surfeit of sadness took me away from the privateers' town for some time. My need to forget was worsened by a difficult Court case involving maritime law. It was a sordid affair and no light was ever thrown on it. Indeed, it was reminiscent of the worst malpractices of the great trading deals of days long gone. I fell victim to a law dating from the days of Vauban which, ironically enough, was passed originally to prohibit these very deals. I was financially ruined and forced to alter a career which I had hoped would be of a higher cultural quality. The ceaseless untiring tides of the passing years, though, have almost erased the memories of an adversity that was, perhaps, necessary.

76

The Merchant Navy College overlooking the town walls.

It was Loïc Frémont who had the idea, in 1972, of asking me to give a poetry recital in the courtyard of the castle. This was an opportunity to enjoy an invigorating stay in Saint-Malo with my younger children, Manuel and Fiona, and my new wife, Lydie, whom I had got to know in Israel, thanks to my eternal love of travelling and a particularly intense period in my life. I met up with old friends (I was to see them again, later, when they "came up" to Paris for a television programme bringing together all my old friends and colleagues) and was fortunate enough to make new friends who gathered in La Gouesnière, in a warm, friendly old residence in which liberty, fervour and poetry roam unrestricted. Parodying Ecclesiastes, I could say that there was time for knowing. As far as famous sons of Saint-Malo are concerned, I had to admit that, apart from a few exceptions, it was not during my adolescence in the town that I learnt much about the fabulous destiny of some of them. Perhaps because I have always had the habit of taking books with me when visiting countries and learning about their history, I have to admit that it was in Canada that I really got to know Jacques Cartier. It was on the shores of the St. Lawrence that I was able to take stock of the genius of this great man of Saint-Malo. Having gone to sea at a very early age, he received orders from the sovereign and set

Left to right : **Jacques Cartier on the Holland Bastion, a figurehead, and a statue of Duguay-Trouin** *(museum).*

off from Saint-Malo in 1535. It took three expeditions before he finally discovered Canada. It was when I saw the ice on the St. Lawrence, noticed the distance between Quebec and Montreal that he wanted to undertake in a rowing boat, and looked at the Lachine Rapids, that I realised just how superhuman this navigator was. He had opened the way for Champlain and an unsuspected uplifting adventure. And even now, as I stroll through the narrow streets and along the promenades of old Quebec, my heart beats even more strongly than usual, in amazement. The architect of the Quebec fortifications was, after all, a follower of Vauban.

The destiny of Duguay-Trouin, who acquired very early on in life his temerity and culture, is worthy of a mythological hero. His victories, won as a result of his unbelievable audacity and his maritime genius, were encouraged by a decree signed by Pontchartrain legalising privateering, a sort of piracy that became mandatory in the face of strong competition on the high seas over several hundreds of years from Britons, Dutchmen and Portguese. It was this same minister who gave official blessing to a trade that had long been practised in other French ports and that was given the delightful name "ebony wood". In fact, the expression covered the slave trade which brought wealth to the shipowners of Saint-Malo for many years. The Church shut its eyes, Islam in Africa encouraged it, and the king gave it its nobility. Duguay-Trouin, though, was not of this kind. Although he took full advantage of his status as a privateer, he always behaved chivalrously.

While staying in Brazil, I made the acquaintance, a frequent occurrence wherever I have been in the world, of a man from Saint-Malo, a millionaire adventurer who asked me to make a film about the epic capture of Rio da Janeiro by Duguay-Trouin. I wrote to Théo Briant and asked him to sketch out the basis for a plot. The budget was so high that it came to nothing. But it was there, in Rio, during the feverish carnival period, that I learnt about the true grandeur of this navigator from Saint-Malo whose statue I had seen but paid little attention to during my childhood.

When I was younger, too, the name of Mahé de La Bourdonnais meant nothing to me except the name of a street. I discovered the fabulous, exemplary life of this man who, having put to sea at the age of 11, became a determined builder of the French East India Company, and one of its heroes. I learned of his life during a stay on Ile Bourbon and, more particularly, on Ile de France (now known as Réunion and Mauritius respectively). Here, on Mauritius, in the midst of the Grapefruit Botanic Gardens, visitors can still see the admirable house in which the man of Saint-Malo lived with his family. He had come to the island to restore law and order, and to lay out a canal, roads, pontoons, and farmland, all of which he achieved with a work force of two hundred and fifty men who were taken on in Saint-Malo. These men were so hard-working that they used tamed bulls in place of the horses they required but did not have. After completing this enormous task, Mahé de La Bourdonnais continued warmongering and ensured that French genius was triumphant. He remains one of the least well-known of Saint-Malo's sons, a fate that is totally unjust.

There are, though, others such as La Mettrie (1709-1751), a doctor and philosopher, who is unknown in France but whose work had the effect of a time bomb in Holland and Germany. His books and theories have yet to become widely known (Epicureanism and the Man-Machine).

Maupertuis (1698-1759), a mathematician, was recognised at his true worth in Germany and Basle, where he died. Like La Mettrie, he was also the target of attack by Voltaire, which is, in many cases, more than an honour; it is a consecration.

The most popular figure in our youth was undoubtedly Surcouf, not only because he had become a legend in his own right but because his descendents still lived in the town, and do to this day. Although the town's proud motto, "Neither Frenchman nor Breton, I am a man of Saint-Malo", was applicable to many a privateer, it was perhaps best-suited of all to Surcouf. He was an outstanding sailor, full of challenge, a blend of the most daring insanity and the strongest possible sense of his own interest, and his life is an admirable illustration of France's destiny on the high seas. During the French Revolution, which prohibited the slave trade, he carried on, secretly. He then fought the English, as an invincible privateer, became his own shipowner, and again carried out acts of piracy against the English. After the fall of the Napoleonic Empire, he gave himself over entirely to maritime trade, becoming the richest shipowner in France. And there is not a distant land in the tropics, be it in the Indian Ocean or the Gulf of Bengal, where he did not make a triumphant appearance.

Broussais (1772-1838), who is the least-known of all in Saint-Malo and elsewhere (and I think, without being very knowledgeable about medicine, justifiably) was a former privateer-surgeon. He established and strongly, if eloquently, stated a theory of physiological medicine containing errors that were clearly proven in his own day by the progress made by Laennec. His despotic obstinacy was his own downfall.

Much more deserving and upsetting was the fate of Lamennais. He was puny in stature but fervent in his beliefs, and was probably convinced of his message, filled with a vision of the disorders caused by the Reign of Terror, which he could see from his window in the Rue Saint-Vincent, just one hundred yards from

The statue of Surcouf on the Cavalier Bastion.

Chateaubriand's residence. Despite their differences, these two geniuses have somehow come together in a form of romanticism that has left traces even today. A book describing the relationship between these two contemporaries in Saint-Malo, who were so close yet so different, would be an enthralling work. And a synthesis of their two lines of thought might be helpful for those whose spiritual adventures remove them from material antagonism and for whom tolerance is a source of rapturous emotion. It would be preferable for the synthesis to be written in the style of Chateaubriand, with an intelligence that is musical in expression. I have travelled through many countries, I have felt the attraction of many a town, have even, in some instances, been subjected to their powers. I am convinced that there are towns which enjoy a particularly privileged geographical position on the surface of the globe, and that their natural antagonism has become a dialogue with the natural environment of ocean, forest, mountain, and desert, not forgetting their place compared to the great mysterious stars of the firmament. These sites have been blessed by gods whom the prophets have forgotten and neglected, but to whom History pays tribute, telling of what they once were - and still are today. I cannot list all these promontory towns, ports of call on maritime or cosmic routes. I have felt messages that still contained a sense of urgency and magic in places that are falling into decline such as Rome, Luxor, Epidaurus, Angkor, or Baalbek. I have felt still-living calls in Hamburg, Leningrad, and Hong Kong etc. The most troubled, in whose vicinity my life experienced a sort of rebirth, was Jerusalem, the centre of all three monotheistic religions. Yet the town which remains the most obvious for my innermost soul is Saint-Malo to which I now return with increasing frequency to seek solace, since the state of innocence drawn from my childhood and that must last beyond the grave, is becoming more and more urgent, so that, at the end, as I fall asleep for the last time with those who have been dear to me, Serenity and Wisdom, acquired at last for the price that must be paid for all material and spiritual adventures, will leave behind the memory of a man of goodwill.

May all those who pass through this town or the absentminded population living there day after day listen to the psalms of the stones, the hearty laughs or quiet sighs of the waves measuring its dialogue to fit the lunar months, in the coldest but much more eloquent seasons.

Daniel Gélin

Jean Mounier / André Lespagnol

*Saint-Malo - yesterday,
today and tomorrow.*

An aerial view of Saint-Malo.

******* lthough the town is no more than of average
A size as regards its population of just over
50,000, or "49,600 and a few more Malouins"
******* as a journalist put it in May 1990, Saint-Malo
nevertheless enjoys great influence internationally, and it
has a prestigious history. It was, after all, among the
foremost trading ports in Europe and the world as a
whole in the early years of the 18th century.

Finding an explanation for this apparent contradiction in
terms is an intellectual exercise which can help to
understand the Saint-Malo of today and catch a glimpse
of the Saint-Malo of tomorrow. A town's prosperity does
not depend on its size but on the developmental structure
of its original activities and its population's capacity for
innovation. Nowadays, towns are no longer ranked
according to size but rather more on the specificity of
their functions. Saint-Malo, the "daughter of the sea", has
taken full advantage of all that its natural environment
has to offer but has more especially benefitted from the
audacity, spirit of initiative and, in some cases, spirit of
adventure of its sailors and merchants.

In a 20th century plagued by repeated crises, Saint-Malo
no longer has the enormous wealth that it once enjoyed
thanks to its flourishing maritime activities and the
profits from privateering or illicit trading. On several
occasions, Saint-Malo has been forced, to borrow an
expression from Roger Vercel, "to clew up its hopes and
heave to". Yet since the town has managed to change
part of its wealth into an architectural and artistic
heritage and its population has kept its spirit of
competition and its will to succeed, it is legitimate to
hope that the downturn in the general crisis represents,
again quoting Roger Vercel, "the long-awaited brightness
during which one can shake out the sails and set off
again".

A basic advantage : the beauty of a coastal setting

Saint-Malo, daughter of the sea, daughter of the coast, has been endowed by nature with a magnificent costume, like a deep-cut gown trimmed with lace. The finely-indented coastline includes numerous safe havens which are particularly suitable for the creation of natural harbours and which led to the earliest examples of fishing and seafaring.

The coastline has been carved out by the waters of the Channel that have eaten into the edge of the Armorican upland since the climate began to warm up some 10,000 years ago. The rise in sea level when the glaciers began to melt resulted in the four natural features which characterise Saint-Malo and brought it its fortune. Firstly, the sea rose along the deep Rance Valley, laying out a means of access to the hinterland where ships of the sea gave way to river boats. Yet despite the extension of this natural access by the building of the Ille-et-Rance Canal, which was not completed until 1840, the expansion of the inland areas or hinterland was less marked than in the Loire Valley round Nantes, or the Garonne Valley near Bordeaux. Simultaneously, the invading waters cut off several granite outcrops, the largest of which attracted communities of monks, general populations and urban developments e.g. Alet which was Maclow's rock, Cézembre and Mont Saint-Michel. Between these islands and rocky outcrops on the mainland, the sea deposited fine sand in wide bays, creating magnificent beaches or long strings of sand dunes commonly called "sillons". Within the shelter of the most famous of all these dunes, at Rochebonne, a deeper bay formed a longer-lasting area of humidity, a maritime marshland, the shore at Chasles. Irregular sedimentation of sand and mud created a rugged relief in miniature with marshy depressions and higher islets, the famous Talards. It was these tiny islands which, later, made urban development possible, where Rocabey and the railway station district stand today.

Knowledge of these geographical features gives better understanding of the conditions under which the towns of Saint-Servan and Saint-Malo expanded outwards from their isolated rocks. This expansion had to overcome difficulties and obstacles in order to protect the causeway and drain the marshes. Thereafter, it is easy to understand the current layout of the town and the occasional absence of harmony in certain aspects compared to the architectural coherence of the walled town built on the rock.

The charm of the Saint-Malo area is based first and foremost on the beauty of a coastline that constantly changes in appearance according to the movements of the tide. At low water, for example, the rocky coast with its islands and rocks is a constant source of astonishment and admiration. Yet beauty has a price and this living natural environment is also dangerous, for the rocks are also reefs on which boats founder during fierce storms that remain etched in the minds of all who experience them.

Thereafter, man was obliged to master the wrath of the sea. He had to learn how to avoid the treachery of coastline and tides. And this will to gain mastery over nature finally helped to inculcate courage and forge characters. The influence of the physical attraction of the coastline goes some way to explaining the contradictions in the "Saint-Malo soul" that Roger Vercel analysed with such insight. Although, on the rocks at Alet and Saint-Malo, places of isolation, the people acquired the mentality of an insular race, full of independence and

Bon-Secours Beach with the two Bé islands in the distance.

On previous pages
**Grand-Bé and Petit-Bé. In the
distance to the right is the island
of Cézembre.**

The main beach.

argument, "Neither Frenchman nor Breton, I am a man
of Saint-Malo!", they also learned to go beyond the
narrow bounds of their environment and widen their
horizons. The men of Saint-Malo risked adventure, set
out in search of anything new. They had a pioneering
mentality, going ever onwards in the exploration of more
and more distant lands, discovering trade routes that
were increasingly long. Without their courage and will to
succeed, would captains and sailors ever have overcome
the terrible dangers of Cape Horn and survived the
rigours of life as Newfoundland fishermen?

Of course, these traits of character have led to the success
of the town's maritime activities and to its economic
prosperity. They also led to the development of the
surrounding countryside, amidst the rural society of Le
Clos-Poulet. Investment by wealthy townspeople,
openmindedness on the part of the peasants, and a love
of exchanges with foreign countries facilitated the introduction of constantly changing agricultural techniques and
the acceptance of speculative types of crop. It has to be
said that the area enjoys a temperate climate and the
presence of fertile soil. But these same factors are to be
found on the side of the Rance Valley where the
development of agriculture was totally different.

The heritage
of an exceptional history

****

I

****
t was by turning resolutely seawards that people were able to give the island town its importance and international influence, despite the fact that its area was "less than that of the Tuileries Gardens" as Chateaubriand said.

Maritime adventure : the spirit of discovery

Jacques Cartier.

At the dawn of the modern era, the people of Saint-Malo made an eminent contribution to major discoveries and to recognition of the New World.

In the early years of the 16th century, they set out across the North Atlantic, and took part in the exploration of the coasts of North America, from Acadia to Labrador. Tradition has it that they were the discoverers of the island of Cap-Breton. Sailors from Saint-Malo were to be found hard at work along the shores and in the waters off the "New Lands", exploiting the resources provided by the fabulous banks of fish, mainly cod, which had just been discovered. Now, almost five hundred years later, they still head for the same spots.

It was in order to take advantage of this already extensive maritime experience that King François I chose a famous sea captain from Saint-Malo, Jacques Cartier, to lead an expedition that was to set off westwards and seek a direct route to distant Cathay (China), passing the northern end of the obstacle formed by the American continent.

Commandant Charcot.

JEAN-BAPTISTE
1867 CHARCOT 1936

Although he failed in this final objective, which was, in fact, a "mission impossible", the navigator from Saint-Malo succeeded, at the end of his two expeditions (1534 and 1535), both of which had been prepared in Saint-Malo, in discovering the "royal seaway" into the heart of the North-American continent, the vast river which he called St. Lawrence. As he sailed up the waterway to Quebec and Hochelaga (later known as Montreal), he found himself sailing into the heart of the "land of Canada", the future cradle of French colonisation in North America.

Jacques Cartier, the man from Saint-Malo, thus be- came one of the "founding fathers" of Canada and his memory, particularly in his manorhouse at Limoëlou, continues to feed the symbolic and affective "special relationship" between the great North American country, especially its French-speaking population in Quebec, and the town on the R. Rance.

This "spirit of discovery" lasted for many more years in Saint-Malo, reaching a high point in the 18th century when its sailors played an active role in the exploration of the southern areas of the Indian Ocean or the regions around Terra del Fuego. By taking the sea route round Cape Horn in the early years of the 18th century, and they were the first to do so on a regular basis, they made a decisive contribution to the exploration of the great archipelago in the South Atlantic which was to keep, to the present day, as one of its two common names, the "Iles Malouines" (better known in English as the Falkland Islands).

In fact, it was a fairly logical continuation of this tradition that brought Commandant Charcot to Saint-Malo - Saint-Servan at the beginning of this century to establish his home port and point of departure for his voyages of discovery in the polar regions, from Antarctica up to Greenland, until the tragic end of his ship, the *Pourquoi-Pas*, in 1936.

Intellectual adventure

The spirit of adventure and interest in the world at large was also a characteristic feature of the many sons of this maritime town who, from the 18th century onwards, were drawn towards intellectual activities, in the fields of science or literature. Each in his own fashion, this aspect is illustrated by the careers of people like Moreau de Maupertuis, mathematician, who gained fame by measuring the terrestrial meridian in Lapland and who ended his career as President of the Academy of Sciences in Berlin, at the invitation of Frederick II; or François-René de Chateaubriand, who set off on the highways and byways of Europe as a result of the French Revolution, even travelling as far as the edges of the North American forest. The author of Atala drew some of his pre-Romantic inspiration from his travels.

For other great intellectual figures produced by Saint-Malo between 1750 and 1850, the adventure was of a more abstract or spiritual nature. But they, too, were men of character and, in many cases, controversy. Yet they were also men of stature, men like La Mettrie, a materialist philosopher whose views smacked of heresy, Broussais, Doctor and Revolutionary in practice and in his opinions, or Félicité de Lamennais, an intransigeant Catholic turned democrat during the 1848 Revolution. They too helped, through the wide variety of works they produced, to increase the fame of their homeland.

A portrait of Chateaubriand by Girodet-Trioson *(museum).*

Economic adventure : a spirit of enterprise

Even more than the seafarers, however, who carried out their orders, and the intellectuals who were the product of the society that they created, it was the merchants who, for many centuries, brought Saint-Malo its international prestige. The greatest of the merchant families, the Magons, Le Fers, Eons, and Danycans, the "Gentlemen of Saint-Malo" to quote the book of the same name, are true "heroes", little known in Saint-Malo's history yet the creators of its essential grandeur, which was first and foremost economic in origin.

By actively developing maritime trade on a large scale, with long-haul voyages, fitting out ships, exporting cod and canvas, and setting up trading networks with foreign countries, these great businessmen turned Saint-Malo into one of the most enterprising centres of European capitalism of post-mediaeval times, reaching its heyday in the 1700's.

Its dynamic attitudes were evident in the success of privateering, the "continuation of trade by other means", the means in question being force which was used quite legally in times of war for the capture of enemy merchant

Left to right : **The Capture of Rio da Janeiro by Duguay-Trouin,** *by Gudin.* **The Battle of the *Kent* and the *Confiance*,** *by Garneray.*

ships, and which is an excellent expression of the conquering, even aggressive, nature of Saint-Malo's capitalism at that time. There is no better illustration of this than Duguay-Trouin, the man who succeeded in everything he did, with his countless captures of richly-laden English and Dutch ships returning from the Caribbean or the East Indies and the pinnacle of his fame, the victorious attack on Rio da Janeiro in 1711 which was held to ransom for Brazilian gold dust, a means of providing high profits for his shipowners.

Yet the success of the privateers, which was undisputed during the reign of Louis XIV, was by definition temporary and, in many cases, a question of chance, and it should not be allowed to mask the other, equally spectacular examples of the maritime and trading enterprise of Saint-Malo and its people. There was, for example, the extraordinary adventure of the "Southern Seas" which took them, during the first quarter of the 18th century, to the forbidden markets of distant Peru, even though this required the "invention" of the Cape Horn sea route and the facing, and overcoming, of thousands of risks and perils.

A portrait of Surcouf *(anonymous).*

The Battle of the *Cartier* and the *Triton*, *by Trémisot*

Their success was no less important in the other distant setting, the Indian Ocean, from which they provided the transport of goods for a spell (1710-1720) by creating their own East India Company. They left their mark on this area throughout the 18th century, either acting for their own benefit, like the privateer and trader, Robert Surcouf, or in the service of the East India Company. It was a sea captain from Saint-Malo who took possession of the Ile de France (Mauritius) in the king's name in 1715, and it was one of his compatriots, Mahé de La Bourdonnais, a man of boundless energy, who turned it into a prosperous colony, and a centre for trade with the Indian Ocean. Memories of

The Château du Bos.

this man are still very much alive there today, in stone and soil.

It was the dazzling successes in privateering, blockade-running and trading with India that created the colossal fortunes which were turned into the town houses, and the country houses known as "malouinières", built during the first half of the 18th century.

Integration into the European economy

Yet, quite apart from these brilliant but often short-lived episodes, trade in Saint-Malo developed in the long term on more prosaic grounds, as a basic part of exchanges within the European economy.

Starting with the export of farm produce and, more especially textiles (canvas) from the Breton hinterland, the people of Saint-Malo built up their trade links both with Southern Europe (Iberian Peninsula from Bilbao to Alicante, and more particularly the ports of And-alusia such as Seville and Cadiz, the gateways to the rich Spanish-American markets) and North-Western Europe, i.e. the Netherlands and Holland and, first and foremost, the British Isles, usually Southern England and Ireland, which were within a sail's length of their ramparts. By achieving a complex balance between the "Spanish trade" and the "English trade", Saint-Malo established itself for many years as a link in the Atlantic Arc, long before such a thing existed, providing a maritime connection between the most enterprising economic centres of North-Western and Southern Europe.

A privileged link with Britain

A very special relationship existed, though, with the great neighbour to the north, Britain, which, by one of the hazards of History, traded with the Channel

The carved rocks in Rothéneuf.

Islands of Jersey and Guernsey only a few nautical miles away.

Links with Southern Europe gradually faded after the Revolutionary and Napoleonic Wars, but, after the ups and downs of the second major Franco-English conflict (the "Second One Hundred Years' War from 1689 to 1815), Saint-Malo regained its fundamental purpose as the "gateway to England" achieved as a result of its geographical situation and ar age-old history dating back to the days of the Celts.

After Waterloo, the innate link with the great island neighbour was gradually re-established, and was facilitated by the means of transport provided by the industrial era. An illustration of this is the opening of the Southampton-Saint-Malo steamer link in 1845. And it was further strengthened, after 1860, by the Franco-English Free Trade Agreement. Thus, in the second half of the 19th century, Saint-Malo again became one of the main gateways to the English market which was particularly interested in the farm produce of Western France, starting with the vegetables from Le Clos-Poulet. Inversely, its wet docks, which had finally been completed, saw massive imports of Welsh coal, the new "industrial bread" for Western France.

This vital link with England brought with it increasing numbers of visitors, who were soon to be known as "tourists", all of them endowed with money, free time, and curiosity.With them came subtler influxes - of fashion, lifestyles, and cultural models, all of which could be seen in the style of the hotels and villas, the sudden "blossoming" of tennis courts and golf courses, and the development of yachting.

It was by "going British" that Saint-Malo, and the Saint-Malo region at large, joined the modern tourist industry, as far back as the Edwardian Era (or even *further back, in the 1850's in Dinard, the first British bridgehead), and from Saint-Briac to Rothéneuf the coastal scenery changed, become worthy of its name, the "Emerald Coast". Tourism offered it a new economic advantage that was vital for the future, as long as the area developed its full potential.*

The marina in the Vauban Basin.

A historic town facing up to the future

****

T hus, over the ages, the natural environment and human temperament have created a fine town with an international character. The

****

people are still proud of their community, coastline and countryside. And anybody who has left the area, sometimes for social reasons, has an ever-lasting dream of a final return to the place of his birth. The only problem is that, in these days of technological upheaval, economic changes and social revolutions, a town cannot live on its past. It must now have a dynamic vision of the future and undertake a forward-looking analysis of its development. Fortunately, faced with the advantages created by the likely development of international relations, especially with the setting up of the Single European Market, Saint-Malo and the area round about have several trump cards to play.

The harbour and maritime vocation reborn

Despite the crises which more deeply affect the sector linked to the harbour, it is nevertheless this sector that constitutes the basis for Saint-Malo's development. The reconversion of the fishing fleet, and the development of goods and passenger ferry traffic have revived the harbour bringing in their wake possible economic and social development for the region as a whole.

Nowadays, with numerous difficulties or even downright opposition a thing of the past, the harbour con-

The mouth of the mercantile harbour.

sists of four wet docks built into the cove sheltered by the causeway, the rocks of Saint-Malo and Alet. On site, it is easy to understand the layout of the harbour and the distribution of its functions by looking along the wharves at the various types of boat corresponding to a wide range of maritime activities that are undergoing constant change.

The reconversion of the fishing fleet

Faced with an unfavourable economic climate as a result of a decrease in natural resources and an increase in international regulations, Saint-Malo was obliged to change in order to maintain a minimum hold on the long-haul fishing industry and build up a maximum quantity of fresh catches.

There are those who, quite understandably, speak nostalgically of the forest of masts from several dozen Newfoundland fishing boats (there were ninety of them in the early 1920's) which, in the Duguay-Trouin Basin, stated fairly and squarely Saint-Malo's position as one of the foremost cod fishing ports in France. The employment crisis in this sector is particularly striking when one realises that long-haul fishing no longer employs more than one hundred fishermen for the entire maritime district of Saint-Malo, as opposed to several thousand at the beginning of this century. However, the modernisation of the great trawlers has gone some way towards lessening the rigours of a difficult job done by men from very poor backgrounds who, on the Grand Banks, became veritable "galleyslaves of the fog", to use the poignant description by René Convenant.

Compared to earlier times, the yield from long-haul fishing has not dropped in any noticeable proportions; catches passed from 6,000 tonnes in 1923 to 5,132

In the Duguay-Trouin Basin.

tonnes in 1989. In fact, the main problem is how to maintain, year in year out, the activity of three or four large vessels belonging to Comapêche which, with the dynamic outlook of its managers, is attempting to uphold the economic importance of long-haul fishing, for the decrease in stock and the resulting conflicts with our "cousins" from Canada and Saint-Pierre-et-Miquelon have led to a serious decline in the importance of this type of fishing over the past decade, given that catches had risen to 8,900 tonnes in 1977! With the crisis in employment and production, there was a need to find other forms of fishing, and it became profitable to undertake short trips out to sea or along the coast. This type of fishing, which provides fresh fish and shellfish that are becoming increasingly valuable on the market, brings activity to the Trichet and Val Jetties to the south of the Bouvet Basin. Although expansion has stabilised, under the constraints imposed by European legislation, fresh fishing has now reached the same level as long-haul fishing, in quantity and quality, while employing two or three times more men. In all, the maritime district of Saint-Malo has become a busy fishing area again and, as regards employment, has outstripped the Douarnenez-Camaret area. At the same time, Comapêche has done its utmost to increase the perceived

Years	1987			1988			1989		
Mercantile harbours	Lorient	Brest	St Malo	Lorient	Brest	St Malo	Lorient	Brest	St Malo
Total goods landed	2768	1738	1419	2991	1582	1451	3087	1300	1445
Goods landed excl. hydrocarbons	2251	1045	1309	2367	880	1339	2410	631	1300
Goods exported	51	272	273	82	267	241	95	292	299

Commercial business in 1,000 T in the three main ports in the economic region of Brittany - Lorient, Brest and Saint-Malo.
Source material : tables showing the Breton economy, pub. INSEE, Rennes Regional Division.

value of seafood. The company is involved in the production of popular foodstuffs such as surimi, and has set up a company which uses processes that are identical to those developed in Japan. Fishing, then, has retained an important place in the harbour, even though the other sectors are undergoing large-scale expansion.

The extension of the mercantile harbour

Among the major mercantile harbours in the economic region of Brittany, Saint-Malo is well-placed. With its 1.5 million tonnes, it follows Lorient (2.9 million tonnes) and Brest (1.7 million tonnes) for goods landed, but it overtakes Brest as regards imports excluding hydrocarbons, and exports of goods are four or five times higher here than in Lorient.

This result is based mainly on the development of the chemicals industry, specialising in the production of fertilisers using the seams of marl on the seabed in the Channel. Marl is a marine sediment consisting of calcareous algae. The production is also based on the use of phosphates and potash, which are imported directly through the harbour in Saint-Malo where the modern unloading equipment and storage facilities can be seen on the wharves in the Vauban and Jacques-Cartier Basins.

The industry, which was originally based on the transformation of a product from the sea, has expanded thanks to the dynamism of the Timac Company which, with more than 550 employees, is the biggest chemicals company in Brittany. Its success has led to the setting up of an efficient industrial group, the Groupe Roullier, which, in the fertilisation sector, "ranks first among privately-owned French companies and twelfth in Europe". The Groupe Roullier has div-

**The harbour equipment
on the Corsaires Wharf.**

The four factory trawlers of the Comapêche Company. It is extremely unusual to seem them all in at the same time in the Duguay-Trouin Basin.

ersified its production in Brittany and set up subsidiaries throughout the world, reinforcing the international influence of Saint-Malo. Using an interactive image, one can say that Saint-Malo Harbour has made Timac, and that Timac woke up Saint-Malo Harbour. Here, as in fishing, an enterprising spirit based on the perceivable worth of maritime activities has led to the development of other industrial sectors. New companies transform marine algae into dietetic or pharmaceutical products, using high tech resulting from R & D that ensures the company international competitivity. The Goëmar Company, for example, which is of modest size with some one hundred employees in Saint-Malo, has set up companies in the United States and created commercial subsidiaries in China and Japan where it signed technical cooperation agreements with the famous large group, Mitsubishi. In the same way, the Codif-Phytomer Laboratories have acquired recognised skill in the production of algae-based growth correctors.

Finally, the difficulties experienced by the shipbuilding industry are beginning to be overcome thanks to a

spirit of innovation based on high tech and the use of new materials. In this field, a number of companies are again making use of wood and a skilful use of plastics. Morgere has begun the production of a new dragnet; others introduce different new products based on research developed by Ifremer and designed to ensure the economic viability of fishing without destroying the ecological balance.

The boom in passenger transport

In 1989, more than 900,000 travellers passed through Saint-Malo Harbour, which is now the busiest Breton ports as regards passenger transport. It is true that just over one-half of the traffic consists of tourists travelling to the Channel Islands. Yet in just ten years, passengers travelling to and from England have more than doubled, passing from 200,000 in 1977 to 450,000 in 1989! There are many who have spoken of the return of the British to the continent. The success of this sector is due to the work of the BAI, a company with a head office in Roscoff which succeeded in strengthening the structure of Saint-Malo as a harb-

The Rance Tidal Power Station.

Opposite, left :
On the Surcouf Wharf.

Right :
The *Grande-Hermine*, the latest addition to the Comapêche fleet.

our. The ferry links, in particular with Portsmouth, carry passengers and cars, and lorries providing commercial links with Britain. More rarely do the lorries travel from Britain to Spain.

This maritime function should, within the framework of a united Europe, enjoy a promising future, for at present, according to the study undertaken by Mr. Phliponneau, the harbours of Brittany have only a very small share of cross-Channel business : 6.8% of passengers and only 1.8% of lorry traffic, compared to 15.4% and 12.3% for the harbours in Lower Normandy.

Yet Saint-Malo is the end of the shortest road from Spain. Saint-Malo is one of the vital elements in the regions of the Atlantic Arc that are attempting to counterbalance the weight of highly-developed regions along the Rhine axis. It is easy to see why extension and deepening of the harbour is necessary, as demanded by the political and economic leaders of the town and the region as a whole. The commercial trade routes through Europe must be brought through Saint-Malo, long before most of the traffic is finally fixed by the Estuary Motorway and Chunnel route.

The required extension of the harbour is also a trump card in the development and evolution of tourism.

Tourism : a changing world

The importance of tourism in the Saint-Malo area can be defined in a few statistics which are not always easy to scale down to the urban district. There are somewhat over one hundred hotels, with an occupancy rate of the order of 70% in 1989. Rather more than 50,000 people spent some time in the summer on municipal campsites, and there are 5,000 holiday homes. In the district as a whole, more than 4,000

Enjoyment on the beach.

people are employed directly in activities linked to tourism, for the industry is not restricted to the town itself. It has taken on a regional dimension, extending right along the Emerald Coast, from the Baie du Mont Saint-Michel to Cap Fréhel. There is no doubt that, if the Emerald Coast has increased Saint-Malo's fame, the attraction of this part of the shoreline is due as much to its natural charms as to the presence of Saint-Malo. Within this geographical combination, seaside holidays still have an important place during the holiday period. Situated as it is on the Channel seaboard, the Emerald Coast enjoys several advantages that are far from negligeable e.g. beautiful scenery, a sunnier climate, and the highest sea temperature anywhere along the Channel coast. Yet seaside holidays are not

The start of the 1986 edition of the *Route du Rhum* transatlantic yacht race.

**The Château des Chênes,
now the music school.**

Remains of the cathedral cloisters.

restricted to lazing on the beach; they always include increasingly-attractive sports activities such as tennis, golf etc. Above all, sailing is particularly well catered for thanks to the recent setting up of harbour amenities making Saint-Malo the foremost yachting marina in Brittany and a top-ranking centre in France for major nautical competitions on a national and international level.

Yet it should not be thought that tourists visiting the Saint-Malo area today are content to do no more than acquire an unintelligent suntan. Over the past few years, tourism has become more active, thanks to a number of factors.

First of all, there is increased mobility, with trips through the area, drives along each side of the Rance and across the dam whose economic importance is not limited to the mere production of a far from negligeable quantity of electricity. The tourism for health sector is due to expand with the now certain success of marine hydrotherapy that attracts large numbers of people to the Thermes in Saint-Malo and is further strengthened by the recent opening of another centre in Dinard. In particular, though, efforts have been made to introduce a cultural form of tourism, with the provision of cultural events and historical shows, and the organisation of guided tours to museums, castles, and "malouinières" designed to draw the attention of holidaymakers to the past and the high-quality heritage of the Saint-Malo area. This cultural tourism is being overtaken by business tourism, based on meetings and conferences for economic decision-makers.

It is by the combination of all these factors that the Saint-Malo area can hope to increase the influx of summer visitors and, more importantly, extend the season. And it is true that increasing numbers of tourists from Mediterranean regions are mainly drawn here by the wide range of cultural attractions in the Saint-Malo area - the organisation of leisure activities for people with "free time" is also based on the cultural interest of travel and the invigorating effects of holidays.

By its natural environment, its past history and its architectural heritage, Saint-Malo is very well able to reconcile three forms of tourism - for leisure, for health and for culture.

An attractive architectural and cultural heritage

It is "a town of artistic and cultural interest built by privateers", as Henri Queffélec described it, and the town draws as many visitors as the beaches and coastline. The recent expansion of the urban district respected the architectural uniqueness of the old, historic town. After the disaster of the Second World War, the rebuilding policy followed by the town's leaders under the efficient guidance of the mayor, Guy La Chambre, made it possible to give back to the walled town the granite houses that had been designed according to principles of majesty in architecture as conceived by an engineer. Rebuilding in the 1950's generally maintained the urban layout and beauty of the stone buildings once designed by Vauban but mainly built by the engineer, Siméon de Garangeau. He it was who, early in the 18th century, made the major extensions to the town thanks to the fortunes of the great merchants who gave Saint-Malo its international dimension.

All these great shipowners' and privateers' houses can be admired by walking round the top of the town walls for which Saint-Malo is famous. Saved from destr-

Looking towards the Dinan Gate.

Items that once belonged to Surcouf (*museum*).

uction during the war, the ramparts offer delighted visitors all the rigour and uniformity of military architecture.

This being so, an attentive tour of Saint-Malo will be of interest both for the knowledge it provides of the past and for the example it gives of a specific style of urban development. Little wonder, then, that at weekends and during the summer, tourists and locals who never tire of the old walled town crowd into the busy shop-lined streets. Of course, in many of the new districts in Paramé or Saint-Servan, especially in Le Rosais and Le Gros Chêne, the architecture in the housing estates is similar to that seen in many other towns in Brittany. Yet originality comes to the fore again in the Madeleine District where recently-built blocks of flats drive out memories of the dismal council housing of years gone by.

Architectural originality can also be seen in the luxurious residences that rich merchants and shipowners had built in the 18th century in the countryside in Le Clos-Poulet and on the shores of the R. Rance. These "malouinières", fine houses of stone and glass separated from the neighbouring fields by long stone walls are veritable little manorhouses filled with the riches, furniture and works of art of that period. Many works and guide books describe dream estates such as the Château du Bos and Château de la Chipeaudière beyond Saint-Servan, the La Mettrie manorhouse in Les Louets and the Le Lupin Mansion beyond Paramé, on the way to Cancale. A sight of these houses brings to life the history of the success of a social class and maintains respect for our heritage, just as visits to the museums in the Saint-Malo area teach us about the history of a town and a whole population. The district has succeeded in setting up numerous memorials to

Saint-Malo Harbour in the early 19th century (*museum*).

the past e.g. the Alet Archaeology Centre, the town's museum of local history and local celebrities in the castle, and the Cape Horner Museum in the Solidor Tower in Saint-Servan.

Culture, however, cannot be confused with worship of the past. It is still being fashioned today, in exchanges through arts events and the extension of intellectual training. Saint-Malo stages ever-increasing numbers of musical events, study workshops and conferences on unusual subjects which enjoy well-established success. It has to be said, though, that in the past Saint-Malo did not always realise the value of acquiring a means to intellectual training on the spot. In the early years of Saint-Malo's period of glory, merchants and seacaptains preferred their sons to learn from experience, seeing at first hand the difficulties of the job, by going to sea as cabin boys or by travelling overseas to work in branches of their companies such as those in Cadiz in Spain. Apart from the opening of a hydrography college, the town failed for many years to provide any training for the professions, and the young people would attend grammar schools and universities in Dinan, Rennes and, more frequently, Paris.

Nowadays, the level of secondary education has more than caught up with the level in the other major towns of Brittany. Moreover, the need to master advanced technologies has brought industrialists into closer contact with science laboratories in Rennes University or national research agencies. The foreseeable development of cultural exchanges on an international level would suggest an increase, in summer months, in the numbers of foreign students who already attend courses in French language and civilisation in large numbers. These courses could

In summer, there is always a lot happening on the Place Chateaubriand.

become the starting point for a major centre for cultural and scientific exchanges, within a university open to current debates, like the summer schools that exist in other prestigious European cities.

History has left the people of Saint-Malo with a rich heritage which goes far beyond a prestigious image and a set of facile cliches, and far beyond the beauty of an outstanding architectural heritage, despite the disaster of 1944. The main legacy of this history is the example of past success based on a spirit of contact (with the sea, the world and other nationalities) and a spirit of enterprise in the widest sense of the term, with a taste for risk, innovation and conquest. There is no doubt that this history carries with it lessons for the future.

Today, the moderate but regular increase in the population since 1975, the beginnings of a fall in unemployment, the renovation of the harbour and the closely-linked industrial activity, and the marked increase in tourism, seem to confirm that the "boat" has set sail again to find its fortune on the sea and by the sea.

The current expansion is an excellent example of regional development based, not on the introduction of external contributions, but most of all on an indication of the true worth of the town's own resources, defined in Saint-Malo by maritime activities and international relations, sectors in which, now as in days gone past, full advantage can be taken of the specific qualities inherent to the character of the people of Saint-Malo.

At the foot of the Ladies Tower at high tide.

The colour plates in this book were taken by Hervé Boulé with the exception of the photograph on pages 40-41 which is by Guy Daniel.

The black and white photographs on pages 15, 17, 19, 20, 26, 28, 33, 38, 39, 43, 44, 47, 48, 50, 53, 59, 62, 68 and 74 come from Daniel Gélin's own collection.

The photographs of Saint-Malo during the Second World War on pages 67, 69, 70 and 73 are part of Patrick Béroul's collection.

The layout is by Philippe Gentil. The illustrations were engraved by Scann-Ouest and the work was printed in June 1991 by the Imprimerie Aubin in Ligugé.

The cover is by Pierre-Etienne Carlier and Dariouch Khaghany.

I.S.B.N. 2.7373.0879.8 - Dépôt légal : juin 1991
N° éditeur : 2192.01.01.06.91